Cook's Corner

Skinny
Slow
Cooking

igloobooks

igloobooks

Published in 2018
by Igloo Books Ltd
Cottage Farm
Sywell
NN6 0BJ
www.igloobooks.com

All imagery: © iStock / Getty Images

STA002 0218
2 4 6 8 10 9 7 5 3 1
ISBN: 978-1-78810-183-7

Cover designed by Nicholas Gage
Interiors designed by Simon Parker
Edited by Jasmin Peppiatt

Printed and manufactured in China

Cook's Corner

Skinny Slow Cooking

Contents

Cook's Corner

Skinny Slow Cooking

Soups

Vegetable soup with pistou

SERVES: 6 | PREP TIME: 5 MINUTES | COOKING TIME: 3 HOURS

INGREDIENTS

1 butternut squash, peeled deseeded and diced

1 red pepper, deseeded and diced

¼ white cabbage, diced

125 g / 4 ½ oz / 1 cup green beans, cut into short lengths

150 g / 5 ½ oz / 1 cup baby broad beans, defrosted if frozen

2 cloves of garlic, finely chopped

600 ml / 1 pint / 2 ½ cups tomato passata

600 ml / 1 pint / 2 ½ cups vegetable stock

75 g / 2 ½ oz Parmesan, in one piece

FOR THE PISTOU

1 clove of garlic, crushed

50 g / 1 ¾ oz / 2 cups basil leaves, chopped

4 tbsp olive oil

METHOD

1. Mix the vegetables with the passata and stock in a slow cooker.

2. Cover the slow cooker and cook on high for 3 hours. Taste the soup and season with salt and pepper.

3. While the soup is cooking, put the pistou ingredients in a small food processor and blitz to a runny pesto consistency.

4. Ladle the soup into six bowls and top each one with a spoonful of pistou.

5. Use a vegetable peeler to shave over the Parmesan and serve immediately.

Sausage, bean and barley soup

SERVES: 6 | PREP TIME: 20 MINUTES | COOKING TIME: 6 HOURS, 30 MINUTES

INGREDIENTS

300 g / 10 ½ oz / 2 cup dried haricot beans, soaked overnight

200 g / 7 oz / 1 cup pearl barley

1 onion, finely chopped

2 cloves of garlic, chopped

2 bay leaves

4 tomatoes, chopped

6 Toulouse sausages, skinned and broken into pieces

2 large handfuls spinach, washed

2 tbsp Parmesan, finely grated

METHOD

1. Drain the beans from their soaking water and put them in a large saucepan of cold water.

2. Bring to the boil and cook for 10 minutes then drain well.

3. Mix the beans with the barley, onion, garlic, bay leaves and sausages in a slow cooker. Pour over enough boiling water to cover everything by 5 cm (2 in), then cook on low for 6 hours or until the beans are tender, but still holding their shape.

4. Season to taste with salt and pepper, then stir in the spinach and cook for a further 30 minutes.

5. Ladle the soup into bowls and sprinkle with Parmesan before serving.

Beetroot soup

SERVES: 2-4 | PREP TIME: 15 MINUTES | COOKING TIME: 2 HOURS

INGREDIENTS

200 g / 7 oz potatoes, peeled and diced

200 g / 7 oz beetroot, peeled and diced

2 tsp olive oil

1 onion, diced

1 celery stick, sliced

1 clove of garlic, minced

750 ml / 25 fl. oz / 3 cups low salt chicken stock

2 sprigs of thyme, leaves chopped

1 bay leaf

275 ml / 9 ⅓ fl. oz / 1 ¼ cup skimmed milk

METHOD

1. Preheat the oven to 180°C (160°C fan) / 350F / gas 4.

2. Place the potatoes and beetroot onto a baking tray and drizzle with a little oil and season. Place into the oven and roast for 1 hour until tender.

3. Heat the remaining oil in a large saucepan. Add the onions and celery and sweat for 5-6 minutes until softened. Add the garlic and cook for a further minute until fragrant.

4. Add the potatoes, beetroot, stock, thyme and bay leaf. Heat until boiling before reducing to a simmer. Cover and leave to cook for a further 45 minutes until tender.

5. Remove the bay leave and blend the soup until smooth using a hand blender. Mix through the milk, you can adjust the amount of milk you add depending on how thick you like your soup.

Mushroom and basil soup

SERVES: 4 | PREP TIME: 10 MINUTES | COOKING TIME: 3 HOURS

INGREDIENTS

1 leek, finely chopped

2 cloves of garlic, crushed

300 g / 10 ½ oz / 4 cups mushrooms, sliced

1 litre / 1 pint 15 fl. oz / 4 cups vegetable stock

100 ml / 3 ½ fl. oz / ½ cup 0 % fat Greek yogurt

1 bunch basil, stems removed

1 small bunch chervil, stems removed

croutons, to serve

METHOD

1. Put the leek, garlic and mushrooms in a slow cooker and pour over the stock.

2. Cover the slow cooker and cook on low for 3 hours.

3. Transfer the soup to a liquidizer and add the yogurt, basil and half the chervil. Blend until smooth.

4. Season to taste with salt and pepper, then ladle into warm bowls and serve garnished with croutons and chervil.

Spinach soup

SERVES: 4 | PREP TIME: 15 MINUTES | COOKING TIME: 3 HOURS

INGREDIENTS

2 leeks, chopped

2 cloves of garlic, crushed

2 potatoes, peeled and diced

1 litre / 1 pint 15 fl. oz / 4 cups vegetable stock

200 g / 7 oz / 6 cups spinach, washed

¼ tsp nutmeg, freshly grated

0 % fat Greek yogurt, to serve

METHOD

1. Put the leeks, garlic and potatoes in a slower cooker and pour over the stock.

2. Cover and cook on medium for 3 hours or until the potatoes start to break down.

3. Stir the spinach into the soup, a couple of handfuls at a time, waiting for it to wilt down before adding the next batch.

4. As soon as it has all been incorporated, transfer the soup to a liquidizer and blend until very smooth.

5. Stir in the nutmeg and season. Serve with a dollop of yogurt.

Cheese and potato soup

SERVES: 2-4 | PREP TIME: 15 MINUTES | COOKING TIME: 6 HOURS

INGREDIENTS

1 onion, diced

2 celery sticks, chopped

2 cloves of garlic, chopped

500 g / 1 lb 1 oz potatoes, peeled and diced

750 ml / 25 fl. oz / 3 cups reduced salt chicken stock

250 ml / 9 fl. oz / 1 cup low fat cream

300 g / 10 ½ oz / 3 cups low fat cheese, grated

ham slices and croutons to serve (optional)

METHOD

1. Preheat the slow cooker to the low setting.

2. Add the onions, celery, potatoes and stock to the slow cooker. Leave to cook for 4 hours until the potatoes are tender.

3. Blend using a hand blender before adding the cream, cheese and seasoning with salt and black pepper.

4. Replace the lid and cook for a further two hours.

5. Serve in bowls topped with the ham and croutons as desired.

Pumpkin soup

SERVES: 6 | PREP TIME: 10 MINUTES | COOKING TIME: 4 HOURS

INGREDIENTS

600 g / 1 lb 5 ½ oz / 3 cups pumpkin or butternut
squash, peeled, deseeded and cut into chunks

1 onion, finely chopped

2 cloves of garlic, finely chopped

1 tbsp fresh thyme, leaves only

1 litre / 1 pint 15 fl. oz / 4 cups vegetable stock

75 ml / 2 ½ fl. oz / ⅓ cup 0 % fat Greek yogurt

2 tbsp pumpkin seeds

METHOD

1. Mix the pumpkin with the onion, garlic and thyme in a slow cooker, then pour over the stock and season well with salt and pepper.

2. Cover the slow cooker and cook on high for 4 hours.

3. Transfer the soup to a liquidizer and blend until smooth. Taste the soup and adjust the seasoning.

4. Pour the soup into warm bowls and top each one with a dollop of yogurt and a sprinkle of seeds.

Asparagus soup

SERVES: 4 | PREP TIME: 10 MINUTES | COOKING TIME: 2 HOURS

INGREDIENTS

450 g / 1 lb asparagus spears, halved and woody ends snapped off

1 leek, finely chopped

2 cloves of garlic, crushed

1 litre / 1 pint 15 fl. oz / 4 cups vegetable stock

150 ml / 5 ½ fl. oz / 2/3 cup 0 % fat Greek yogurt croutons, to serve

METHOD

1. Put the asparagus, leek and garlic in a slow cooker and pour over the stock.

2. Cover the slow cooker and cook on low for 2 hours.

3. Transfer a few asparagus tips to a plate and reserve for the garnish.

4. Transfer the soup to a liquidizer and add the yogurt, then blend until smooth.

5. Season to taste with salt and pepper, then ladle into warm bowls and serve garnished with croutons and the reserved asparagus tips.

Carrot and squash soup

SERVES: 4-10 | PREP TIME: 10 MINUTES | COOKING TIME: 4 HOURS

INGREDIENTS

1 small butternut squash, peeled, deseeded and cut into chunks

2 large carrots, peeled and diced

1 onion, finely chopped

2 cloves of garlic, finely chopped

1 tsp ground coriander seeds

1 litre / 1 pint 15 fl. oz / 4 cups vegetable stock

150 ml / 5 ½ fl. oz / ⅔ cup 0 % fat Greek yogurt

2 tbsp pumpkin seeds

coriander (cilantro) leaves, to garnish

METHOD

1. Mix the squash and carrot with the onion, garlic and ground coriander in a slow cooker, then pour over the stock and season with salt and pepper. Cover and cook on high for 4 hours.

2. Transfer the soup to a liquidizer and blend until smooth. Ripple through the yogurt, then taste the soup and adjust the seasoning.

3. Serve the soup in four large bowls or ten small cups and garnish with pumpkin seeds, coriander leaves and freshly ground black pepper.

19

Vegetable chowder

SERVES: 2-4 | **PREP TIME:** 15 MINUTES | **COOKING TIME:** 1 HOUR

INGREDIENTS

low calorie cooking spray

1 onion, diced

2 carrots, diced

2 celery sticks, diced

3 potatoes, peeled and diced

750 ml / 25 fl. oz / 3 cups low salt chicken stock

1 head of broccoli, florets only

500 ml / 17 fl. oz / 2 cups skimmed milk

1 tsp mace

handful of flat leaf parsley, chopped

1 tbsp cornflour (cornstarch)

METHOD

1. Heat some cooking spray in a large casserole pan over a medium heat. Add the onion, carrots and celery and sweat for 8-10 minutes until softened.

2. Add the potatoes and stock. Heat until boiling before reducing to a low simmer for 30 minutes until the potatoes are tender, add the broccoli to the pan.

3. Heat the milk, mace and parsley in a separate pan. Add to the main chowder and continue to cook for a further 20 minutes.

4. To thicken the chowder, combine the cornflour with a little water to form a paste. Mix this through the chowder to thicken as necessary.

5. Season with pepper and serve.

Minestrone soup

SERVES: 6-8 | PREP TIME: 20 MINUTES | COOKING TIME: 7 HOURS

INGREDIENTS

1.5 l vegetable stock

2 (400g) tins chopped tomatoes

1 large onion, chopped

2 large carrots, diced

1 red pepper, chopped

50 g / half cup of peas

1 small courgette

3 cloves garlic, minced

1 tablespoon fresh parsley

1 ½ teaspoons dried oregano

¾ teaspoon dried thyme

50g any pasta

finely grated Parmesan cheese

METHOD

1. Combine vegetable stock, tomatoes, peas, onion, carrots, courgette, garlic, parsley, oregano, thyme and peppers. Season to taste.

2. Cook in a slow cooker on low for 7 hours.

3. Cook pasta in boiling water, as per manufacturer's instructions, then drain.

4. Stir the pasta into minestrone soup; cook another 15 minutes. Top with Parmesan cheese and garnish of your choice to serve.

French onion soup

SERVES: 4 | PREP TIME: 15 MINUTES | COOKING TIME: 7 HOURS 15 MINUTES

INGREDIENTS

2 tbsp olive oil

3 onions, quartered and sliced

1 tbsp fresh thyme leaves

2 bay leaves

2 cloves of garlic, sliced

1 tbsp balsamic vinegar

1 tbsp runny honey

1 tbsp plain (all-purpose) flour

125 ml/ 4 ½ fl. oz / ½ cup dark ale

1 litre / 1 pint 15 fl. oz / 4 cups vegetable stock

1 baguette, sliced

150 g / 5 ½ oz / 1 ½ cups reduced fat cheese, grated

METHOD

1. Heat the oil in a slow cooker on high for 15 minutes. Stir in the onions, thyme, bay leaves, garlic, balsamic and honey and season well with salt and pepper.

2. Cover and cook on high for 1 hour, stirring every 15 minutes. Stir in the flour, then gradually incorporate the ale and stock, stirring as you go to eliminate any lumps. Cover and cook on low for 6 hours.

3. Taste the soup for seasoning and adjust with salt and pepper, then ladle into bowls. Top the bowls with slices of baguette and sprinkle with cheese, then cook under a hot grill until the cheese has melted and browned.

Cauliflower soup

SERVES: 4 | PREP TIME: 15 MINUTES | COOKING TIME: 3 HOURS

INGREDIENTS

1.2 litres / 2 pints / 4 ¾ cups vegetable stock

1 large cauliflower, chopped

1 large potato, peeled and diced

1 bay leaf

150 ml / 5 ½ fl. oz / ⅔ cup 0 % fat Greek yogurt

50 g / 1 ¾ oz / ½ cup Parmesan, finely grated

¼ tsp nutmeg, freshly grated

METHOD

1. Put the stock, cauliflower, potato and bay leaf in a slow cooker.

2. Cover and cook on low for 3 hours. Discard the bay leaf and reserve a few pieces of cauliflower for a garnish.

3. Ladle the soup into a liquidizer and add the yogurt, Parmesan and nutmeg. Blend until smooth, then season to taste with salt and pepper.

4. Pour the soup into four warm bowls and garnish with the reserved cauliflower and a good grind of black pepper.

Courgette and spinach soup

SERVES: 2-4 | PREP TIME: 10 MINUTES | COOKING TIME: 3 HOURS

INGREDIENTS

1 tsp olive oil

1 onion, diced

2 cloves of garlic, chopped

2 celery sticks, chopped

4 courgettes (zucchini), sliced

1 l / 35 fl. oz / 4 cups low salt vegetable stock

2 potatoes, peeled and diced

200 g / 7 oz spinach, washed

200 ml / 7 fl. oz / ¾ cup low fat crème fraîche

mint to garnish

METHOD

1. Heat the oil in a pan over a medium heat. Add the onions and sauté for 4-5 minutes until soft and translucent.

2. Add the garlic, celery and courgettes and continue to cook for a further 2-3 minutes until fragrant.

3. Transfer to a slow cooker and add the stock, potatoes and spinach. Cook on low for 3 hours until the potatoes are tender.

4. Blend the soup with a hand blender until smooth, mix through the crème fraîche and season with salt and black pepper.

5. Serve in bowls with mint as a garnish and croutons.

Tomato soup

SERVES: 6 | PREP TIME: 10 MINUTES | COOKING TIME: 3 HOURS 30 MINUTES

INGREDIENTS

2 tbsp olive oil

1 onion, finely chopped

2 cloves of garlic, crushed

1 tbsp fresh thyme leaves, plus extra to garnish

1 tbsp concentrated tomato puree

400 g / 14 oz / 2 cups ripe tomatoes, chopped

1 litre / 1 pint 15 fl. oz / 4 cups vegetable stock

2 tbsp flat leaf parsley, chopped

75 ml / 2 ½ fl. oz / ⅓ cup 0 % fat Greek yogurt

METHOD

1. Heat the oil in a slow cooker set to high. Stir in the onion, garlic and thyme, then season with salt and pepper. Cover and cook for 30 minutes, stirring every 10 minutes.

2. Stir in the tomato puree, tomatoes and stock, then cover and cook on low for 3 hours.

3. Transfer the soup to a liquidizer with the parsley and blend until smooth, then pass the soup through a sieve to remove any seeds and bits of skin.

4. Taste for seasoning then ladle the soup into warm bowls or mugs. Stir a little yogurt into each one and garnish with thyme and black pepper.

27

Bacon, beer and cheese soup

SERVES: 4 | PREP TIME: 10 MINUTES | COOKING TIME: 7 HOURS

INGREDIENTS

6 spring onions (scallions), finely chopped, white and green parts separated

1 carrot, finely chopped

1 stick celery, finely chopped

3 rashers smoked streaky bacon, chopped

350 ml/ 12 fl. oz / 1 ½ cup beer

1 litre / 1 pint 15 fl. oz / 4 cups chicken stock

30 g / 1 oz / ¼ cup cornflour (corn starch)

125 ml / 4 ½ fl. oz / ½ cup low fat natural yogurt

250 g / 9 oz / 2 ½ cups reduced fat cheese, grated

METHOD

1. Put the spring onion whites in a slow cooker with the carrot, celery, bacon, beer and chicken stock.

2. Cover and cook on low for 6 hours 45 minutes.

3. Whisk the cornflour into the yogurt, then stir it into the soup.

4. Reserve a handful of cheese to garnish and stir in the rest, then cover and cook for 15 minutes.

5. Taste and adjust the seasoning with salt and pepper, then ladle into bowls and garnish with the spring onion greens and the rest of the cheese.

Thai fish soup

SERVES: 4 | PREP TIME: 5 MINUTES | COOKING TIME: 1 HOUR, 30MINUTES

INGREDIENTS

2 tbsp Thai curry paste

400 ml / 14 fl. oz / 1 ⅔ cups light coconut milk

500 ml / 17 ½ fl. oz / 2 cups fish stock

4 kaffir lime leaves

2 stalks lemongrass

8 spring onions (scallions), cut into short lengths

2 whole sea bass, gutted and scaled

1–2 tbsp fish sauce

1-2 tsp stevia

1 lime, juiced

1 small bunch coriander (cilantro),
roughly chopped

METHOD

1. Stir the curry paste into the coconut milk in
    a slow cooker until dissolved then stir
    in the stock, lime leaves, lemon grass and
    spring onions.

2. Carefully lower in the fish so that they lie in
    a single layer, then cover and cook
    on low for 1 hour 30 minutes.

3. Carefully lift the fish out of the soup with a
    couple of fish slices and transfer to
    a plate. Remove the skin, heads and bones
    and carefully break the flesh into
    large chunks.

4. Season the soup to taste with fish sauce,
    stevia and lime juice, then return the
    fish to the pot.

5. Serve immediately, garnished
    with coriander.

Pork, kale and potato soup

SERVES: 6 | PREP TIME: 20 MINUTES | COOKING TIME: 4 HOURS

INGREDIENTS

2 tbsp olive oil

1 onion, finely chopped

2 cloves of garlic, finely chopped

1 tsp fennel seeds, crushed

4 good quality pork sausages, skinned

4 rashers smoked streaky bacon, chopped

3 medium potatoes, cubed

1 litre / 1 pint 15 fl. oz / 4 cups vegetable stock

150 g / 5 ½ oz / 4 ½ cups curly kale, stems removed and torn into bite sized pieces

150 ml / 5 ½ fl. oz / ⅔ cup low fat natural yogurt

METHOD

1. Heat the oil in a frying pan and fry the onion over a low heat for 10 minutes. Increase the heat to medium and add the garlic, fennel, sausage and bacon.
   Stir-fry for 5 minutes or until the sausagemeat colours a little.

2. Scrape everything into a slow cooker and add the potatoes and stock.

3. Cover the slow cooker and cook on high for 4 hours. Add the kale halfway through.

4. Turn off the slow cooker and remove the inner cooking pot. Stir in the yogurt, then season to taste with salt and pepper.

5. Ladle into six bowls and serve immediately.

Cook's Corner

Skinny Slow Cooking
Meat and fish

Spanish chicken bake

SERVES: 4 | PREP TIME: 5 MINUTES | COOKING TIME: 6 HOURS

INGREDIENTS

200 g / 7 oz / 1 cup canned tomatoes, chopped

1 clove of garlic, crushed

½ tsp smoked paprika

1 yellow pepper, deseeded and sliced

150 g / 5 ½ oz / 1 cup cherry tomatoes, halved

1 handful black olives

4 chicken drumsticks

2 tbsp sundried tomato paste

a few sprigs of rosemary

2 tbsp olive oil

METHOD

1. Tip the canned tomatoes into a small slow cooker and stir in the garlic, paprika and ½ a teaspoon of salt. Arrange the peppers, cherry tomatoes and olives on top.

2. Spread the chicken drumsticks with the sundried tomato paste and lay them on top, then scatter over the rosemary and drizzle with oil.

3. Cover and cook on medium for 6 hours or until the chicken is very tender.

4. Season to taste with salt and pepper before serving.

Cottage pie

SERVES: 6 | PREP TIME: 30 MINUTES | COOKING TIME: 5 HOURS

INGREDIENTS

2 tbsp olive oil

1 onion, finely chopped

2 cloves of garlic, crushed

1 tbsp fresh thyme, stalks removed,
plus extra to garnish

450 g / 1 lb / 2 cups minced beef

400 g / 14 oz / 1 ¾ cups canned tomatoes, chopped

200 ml / 7 fl. oz / ¾ cup beef stock

FOR THE TOPPING

450 g / 1 lb floury potatoes, peeled and cubed

150 ml / 5 ½ fl. oz / ⅔ cup skimmed milk

50 g / 1 ¾ oz / ½ cup reduced fat Cheddar, grated

METHOD

1. Heat the oil in a large frying pan and fry the onion for 10 minutes, stirring occasionally. Add the garlic and thyme and cook for 2 minutes, then add the mince.

2. Fry the mince until it starts to brown then scrape the mixture into a slow cooker and add the tomatoes and stock.

3. Cover the slow cooker and cook on medium for 5 hours.

4. Near the end of the cooking time, cook the potatoes in water for 12 minutes then drain well. Return the potatoes to the saucepan. Add the milk. Mash until smooth.

5. Transfer the cooked mince to a serving dish and top with mashed potatoes and cheese. Cook under a hot grill for a few minutes to brown the top, then serve, garnished with thyme.

Sausage and vegetable casserole

SERVES: 6 | PREP TIME: 10 MINUTES | COOKING TIME: 3 HOURS

INGREDIENTS

1 tbsp olive oil

6 good quality sausages

1 onion, finely chopped

2 sticks celery, diced

2 carrots, sliced

2 cloves of garlic, sliced

1 tsp smoked paprika

150 g / 5 ½ oz / ¾ cup green lentils

400 g / 14 oz / 2 cups canned tomatoes, chopped

1 handful coriander (cilantro) leaves

METHOD

1. Heat the oil in a large frying pan and brown the sausages all over.

2. Transfer to a slow cooker and stir in the rest of the ingredients, except for the coriander. Fill up the tomato can with water and stir it in.

3. Cover and cook on medium for 3 hours.

4. Taste the stew for seasoning and adjust with salt and pepper.

5. Ladle into warm bowls and serve garnished with coriander.

Prawn stuffed peppers

SERVES: 6 | PREP TIME: 5 MINUTES | COOKING TIME: 3 HOURS

INGREDIENTS

1 red onion, finely chopped

150 ml / 5 ½ fl. oz / ⅔ cup dry white wine

3 red peppers, halved and deseeded

150 g / 5 ½ oz / 1 cup cherry tomatoes, chopped

225 g / 8 oz / 1 ½ cups raw prawns (shrimps), peeled

75 g / 2 ½ oz / ½ cup feta cheese, crumbled

2 tbsp flat leaf parsley, chopped

METHOD

1. Sprinkle the onion in an even layer in the base of a slow cooker and pour over the wine. Arrange the peppers on top, cut side up, and fill with tomatoes, prawns, feta and parsley. Season with salt and pepper.

2. Cover and cook on medium for 2 hours or until the peppers are tender.

41

Waterbath lamb chops

SERVES: 2 | PREP TIME: 10 MINUTES | COOKING TIME: 3 HOURS 5 MINUTES

INGREDIENTS

4 lamb chops

2 sprigs rosemary, plus extra to garnish

2 cloves of garlic, unpeeled and squashed

2 tbsp olive oil

6 mushrooms, halved

METHOD

1. Season the lamb chops with salt and pepper then put them in a zip-lock freezer bag with the rosemary, garlic and oil. Seal the bags, excluding as much air as possible.

2. Put the bag in a slow cooker and weigh it down with a plate. Add enough water to cover the lamb by 5 cm (2 in) and set the temperature to low. Cook for 3 hours.

3. Use a thermometer to ensure the water temperature doesn't exceed 60°C (140F) and turn off the slow cooker if needed. Remove the lamb from the bag and blot dry with kitchen paper.

4. Heat a griddle pan until smoking hot, then griddle the lamb and mushrooms for 2 minutes on each side to sear.

Prawn and vegetable curry

SERVES: 4 | PREP TIME: 5 MINUTES | COOKING TIME: 2 HOURS 15 MINUTES

INGREDIENTS

2 tbsp Thai green curry paste

400 ml / 14 fl. oz / 1 ⅔ cups light coconut milk

200 ml / 7 fl. oz / ¾ cup fish stock

1 carrot, crinkle cut

1 small aubergine (eggplant), cubed

150 g / 5 ½ oz / 1 cup green beans, cut into short lengths

1 red pepper, quartered and sliced

1 courgette (zucchini), crinkle cut

1–2 tbsp fish sauce

2–3 tsp caster (superfine) sugar

300 g / 10 ½ oz / 2 cups raw king prawns, peeled with tails left intact

METHOD

1. Stir the curry paste into the coconut milk in a slow cooker until dissolved then stir in the stock.

2. Add the vegetables, then cover and cook on low for 2 hours.

3. Season to taste with fish sauce and caster sugar, then stir in the prawns.

4. Cover and cook for 15 minutes, then serve immediately with steamed rice.

Toad in the hole

SERVES: 4 | PREP TIME: 15 MINUTES | COOKING TIME: 1 HOUR 30 MINUTES

INGREDIENTS

2 tbsp cold pressed rapeseed oil

4 large good quality sausages

100 g / 3 ½ oz / ⅔ cup plain (all-purpose) flour

2 large eggs

175 ml / 6 fl. oz / ⅔ cup skimmed milk

1 tbsp parsley, chopped

METHOD

1. Heat 1 ½ tablespoons of oil in the slow cooker on high for 30 minutes. Swirl to coat the base and 5 cm (2 in) up the sides. Heat the rest of the oil in a frying pan and brown the sausages all over.

2. Put the flour in a large jug with a pinch of salt, then whisk in the eggs and milk. Season with salt and pepper. Take the lid off the slow cooker and immediately pour in the batter. Space out the sausages, then put the lid back on as soon as possible.

3. Cook on high for 1 hour or until well risen. The batter should be fully cooked round the edges and still just a little squidgy beneath the sausages. Sprinkle with parsley.

Pulled pork

SERVES: 8 | PREP TIME: 12 MINUTES | MARINATE: 12 HOURS | COOKING TIME: 10 HOURS

INGREDIENTS

1.8 kg / 4 lb pork shoulder joint, from the collar end

2 tbsp barbecue seasoning mix

2 tbsp olive oil

250 ml / 9 fl. oz / 1 cup chicken stock

salad and sauerkraut, to serve

METHOD

1. Rub the pork all over with the barbecue seasoning, then leave to marinate in the fridge overnight.

2. Heat the oil in a frying pan and sear the pork all over until nicely coloured.

3. Transfer the pork to a slow cooker and pour in the stock.

4. Cover and cook on low for 10 hours.

5. Shred the pork into the stock with two forks and serve with salad and sauerkraut.

Pulled lamb burgers

SERVES: 8 | PREP TIME: 12 MINUTES | MARINATE: 12 HOURS | COOKING TIME: 10 HOURS

INGREDIENTS

1 tsp ground fennel seeds

1 tsp dried oregano

1 tsp dried mint

1 tsp ground cumin

3 cloves of garlic, crushed

2 tbsp soft brown sugar

2 tbsp smoked sea salt

1.8 kg / 4 lb boneless lamb shoulder joint

2 tbsp olive oil

250 ml / 9 fl. oz / 1 cup beef stock

8 burgers buns, halved horizontally

METHOD

1. Mix the fennel, oregano, mint, cumin and garlic with the sugar and salt. Rub the mixture all over the lamb, then leave to marinate in the fridge overnight.

2. Heat the oil in a frying pan and sear the lamb all over until nicely coloured.

3. Transfer the lamb to a slow cooker and pour in the stock. Cover and cook on low for 10 hours.

4. Shred the lamb into the stock with two forks and serve in burger buns with plenty of salad, coleslaw and garlic mayonnaise.

Roast lamb shoulder

SERVES: 8 | PREP TIME: 15 MINUTES | MARINATE: 12 HOURS | COOKING TIME: 8 HOURS

INGREDIENTS

2 mild red chillies (chilies), chopped

3 cloves of garlic, chopped

6 sundried tomatoes in oil

1 tbsp fresh rosemary, chopped

1 tsp fennel seeds, crushed

1.8 kg / 4 lb boneless lamb shoulder joint

2 tbsp olive oil

250 ml / 9 fl. oz / 1 cup dry white wine

METHOD

1. Put the chillies, garlic, tomatoes, rosemary and fennel in a food processor, or pestle and mortar, with a pinch of salt and pepper and blend to a paste. Rub the mixture all over the lamb, then leave to marinate in the fridge overnight.

2. Heat the oil in a frying pan and sear the lamb all over until nicely coloured.

3. Transfer the lamb to a slow cooker and pour in the wine. Cover and cook on low for 8 hours.

4. Transfer the lamb to a carving board, cover with a double layer of foil and leave to rest for 15 minutes. Carve into thick slices and serve.

47

Sweet and sour pork chops

SERVES: 2 | PREP TIME: 10 MINUTES | COOKING TIME: 1 HOUR

INGREDIENTS

4 pork chops, fat scored

2 cloves of garlic, minced

1 tsp fruit syrup

1 tsp red wine vinegar

1 tsp paprika

1 tsp cayenne

100 g / 3 ½ oz vine ripened cherry tomatoes

1 red onion

handful of flat leaf parsley, chopped

METHOD

1. Preheat the oven to 160°C (140°C fan) / 325F / gas 3.

2. Place the chops into a roasting tray.

3. Whisk together the garlic, fruit syrup, vinegar, paprika and cayenne. Season with salt and black pepper. Pour over the chops and toss to coat.

4. Roast in the oven for 1 hour. Add the tomatoes and onion to the roasting pan for the final 20 minutes.

5. Serve with the chopped parsley and salad.

Beef stew

SERVES: 2-4 | PREP TIME: 20 MINUTES | COOKING TIME: 4 HOURS

INGREDIENTS

2 tbsp olive oil

500 g / 1 lb 1 oz lean beef, diced

1 onion, roughly chopped

1 tbsp flour

4 carrots, sliced

750 ml / 25 fl. oz / 3 cups low salt beef stock

4 potatoes, cubed

2 sprigs of thyme

METHOD

1. Heat the oil in a heavy bottomed casserole pan over a high heat and add the beef. Cook for 2 minutes to brown the meat before removing with a slotted spoon.

2. Add the onion and carrots to the pan and fry for 3-5 minutes until starting to brown at the edges. Return the beef and any juices that have been collected to the pan and stir through the flour.

3. Pour the stock into the pan and add the potatoes and thyme. Increase the heat until boiling before transferring to a slow cooker.

4. Cook on the low setting for 4-6 hours, until the beef is soft and vegetables are tender.

49

Rassolnik

SERVES: 2-4 | PREP TIME: 20 MINUTES | COOKING TIME: 1 HOUR 30 MINUTES

INGREDIENTS

low calorie cooking spray

1 onion, diced

2 carrots, diced

2 celery sticks, sliced

4 cloves of garlic, chopped

1 l / 35 fl. oz / 4 cups low salt chicken stock

400 g / 14 oz chicken breast, thinly sliced

1 bay leaf

4 large gherkins, chopped

2 potatoes, peeled and diced

100 g / 3 ½ oz pearl barley

100 ml / 3 ½ fl. oz / ½ cup reduced fat soured cream

METHOD

1. Spray the oil into a large pan and place on a low to medium heat. Add the onions, carrots and celery and sweat for 8-10 minutes.

2. Add the garlic and cook for a further 1-2 minutes until fragrant before pouring in the stock. Increase the heat until boiling before turning down to a low simmer. Add the chicken, bay leaf, gherkins and potatoes. Cover and cook for an hour until the potatoes are tender. Season.

3. Meanwhile, place the pearl barley into a pan of boiling water. Cook for 20 minutes until tender, drain and rinse with cold water.

4. Stir the pearl barley in and heat through before serving with the soured cream.

50

Lamb and red pepper stew

SERVES: 4 | PREP TIME: 20 MINUTES | COOKING TIME: 6 HOURS

INGREDIENTS

450 g / 1 lb / 2 cups lamb shoulder, cubed

2 tbsp olive oil

1 onion, finely chopped

3 red romano peppers, sliced

2 cloves of garlic, finely chopped

2 tsp fresh root ginger, finely chopped

2 red chillies (chilies), chopped

1 tsp paprika

1 tsp ground cumin

2 tbsp tomato puree

600 ml / 1 pint / 2 ½ cups lamb or vegetable stock

METHOD

1. Season the lamb all over with salt and pepper. Heat the oil in a frying pan and sear the lamb on all sides, then transfer the pieces to a slow cooker.

2. Fry the onion and peppers in the frying pan for 5 minutes, then stir in the garlic, ginger and chillies and fry for another 5 minutes. Scrape the mixture into the slow cooker and add the spices, tomato puree and stock.

3. Cover and cook on medium for 6 hours, then adjust the seasoning with salt and pepper.

4. Ladle into warm bowls to serve.

Paella

SERVES: 4 | PREP TIME: 25 MINUTES | COOKING TIME: 2 HOURS

INGREDIENTS

1 litre / 1 pint 15 fl. oz / 4 cups fish stock

pinch of saffron

50 ml / 1 ¾ fl. oz / ¼ cup olive oil

1 onion, finely chopped

1 red pepper, finely chopped

2 cloves of garlic, crushed

200 g / 7 oz / 1 cup paella rice

100 ml / 3 ½ fl. oz / ½ cup dry sherry

8 raw king prawns

8 green-lip mussels

8 clams

lemon wedges, to serve

METHOD

1. Heat the stock in a saucepan with the saffron, but don't let it boil.

2. Heat the olive oil in a frying pan and fry the onion and peppers over a low heat for 15 minutes, stirring occasionally. Add the garlic and cook for 2 minutes, then add the rice and stir over a low heat for 3 minutes to toast it slightly. Add the sherry and simmer until almost completely evaporated.

3. Scrape the contents of the pan into a slow cooker and add the hot stock. Season with salt and pepper and stir well, then cover and cook on high for 1 hour 45 minutes.

4. Press the prawns, mussels and clams down into the rice, then cover and cook for another 15 minutes or until the shells have opened and the prawns have turned pink.

5. The paella can be served straight from the slow cooker. Alternatively, transfer it to a paella pan and brown for a few minutes under a hot grill. Serve with lemon wedges.

Steak and swede slice

SERVES: 4 | PREP TIME: 45 MINUTES | COOKING TIME: 3 HOURS

INGREDIENTS

225 g / 8 oz / 1 ½ cups plain (all-purpose) flour

110 g / 4 oz / ½ cup reduced fat baking spread, cubed and chilled

225 g / 8 oz / 1 ½ cups beef skirt, cut into 1 cm (⅓ in) cubes

1 small onion, finely chopped

150 g / 5 ½ oz / 1 ¼ cups swede, peeled and grated

150 g / 5 ½ oz / 1 ¼ cups potato, peeled and grated

METHOD

1. Reserve 1 tablespoon of flour then rub the baking spread into the rest until the mixture resembles fine breadcrumbs. Stir in just enough cold water to bring the pastry together into a pliable dough, then chill for 30 minutes.

2. Roll out the pastry to match the length and twice the width of a large oval slow cooker.

3. Toss the beef with the onion, swede, potato and reserved tablespoon of flour and season generously with salt and pepper. Spread the mixture over one half of the pastry, then fold it other and crimp tightly to seal.

4. Line the slow cooker with a large sheet of greaseproof paper and lower in the steak slice. Cover and cook on high for 1 hour, 30 minutes.

5. Carefully remove the steak slice using the greaseproof paper and turn it over. Lower it back into the slow cooker, then cover and cook for 1 hour, 30 minutes or until the pastry is cooked through.

6. Cut the steak slice into quarters and serve hot or at room temperature.

Creamy chicken with peas

SERVES: 4 | PREP TIME: 20 MINUTES | COOKING TIME: 3 HOURS 30 MINUTES

INGREDIENTS

2 tbsp olive oil

4 chicken thighs, on the bone

3 shallots, finely chopped

225 g / 8 oz / 3 cups button mushrooms, sliced

2 rashers bacon, chopped

2 cloves of garlic, finely chopped

2 tbsp Pernod

500 ml / 17 ½ fl. oz / 2 cups chicken stock

150 g / 5 ½ oz / 1 cup frozen peas, defrosted

75 ml / 1 ¾ fl. oz / ⅓ cup Greek yogurt

METHOD

1. Heat the oil in a frying pan. Season the chicken with salt and pepper, then sear the skin side until golden brown. Set aside.

2. Add the shallots, mushrooms, bacon and garlic to the pan and sauté for 10 minutes or until lightly coloured. Deglaze the pan with the Pernod, then scrape the mixture into a slow cooker.

3. Arrange the chicken on top, skin side up, then cover and cook on medium for 4 hours

4. Stir the peas into the sauce and cook for another 30 minutes.

5. Stir the yogurt into the sauce just before serving to prevent it from splitting, then season to taste with salt and pepper.

Mediterranean chicken stew

SERVES: 2-4 | PREP TIME: 15 MINUTES | COOKING TIME: 1 HOURS

INGREDIENTS

2 tbsp olive oil

600 g / 1 lb 5 oz chicken thighs

1 onion, diced

2 red peppers, roughly sliced

1 tsp smoked paprika

1 bulb of garlic, halved

400 g / 14 oz canned chopped tomatoes

100 g / 3 ½ oz / ⅔ cup black olives

1 bay leaf

METHOD

1. Preheat the oven to 160°C (140°C fan) / 325F / gas 3. Heat the oil in a casserole pan with a lid over a moderate heat. Add the chicken and brown on all sides for 4-5 minutes. Remove from the pan with a slotted spoon.

2. Add the onions and cook for 4-5 minutes, add the peppers and cook for a further 2-3 minutes. Stir through the paprika before returning the chicken to the pan, adding the garlic, tomatoes, olives and bay leaf.

3. Cover and place into the oven for up to 1 hour, removing the lid for the final 15 minutes. Season to taste and serve.

58

Turkey chilli tacos

SERVES: 2-4 | PREP TIME: 15 MINUTES | COOKING TIME: 1 HOUR

INGREDIENTS

1 tbsp olive oil

1 red onion, diced

500 g / 1 lb 1 oz turkey mince

1 tsp chilli (chili) powder

1 tsp smoked paprika

1 tsp ground cumin

1 tsp ground coriander (cilantro)

400 g / 14 oz tinned chopped tomatoes

6 corn taco shells

100 g / 3 ½ oz / 1 cup low fat Cheddar cheese, grated

METHOD

1. Heat the oil over a medium high heat in a large casserole. Add the onion and cook for 6-8 minutes until softened.

2. Add the mince and brown before adding the chilli powder, paprika, cumin and coriander. Fry for a further minute until fragrant. Add the chopped tomatoes and half fill the can with water before adding to the pan, heat until boiling.

3. Turn the heat down to a simmer and cover the pan. Leave to simmer gently for 1 hour.

4. Serve the chilli with the taco shells and cheese.

Cod, broccoli and potato gratin

SERVES: 4 | PREP TIME: 20 MINUTES | COOKING TIME: 3 HOURS

INGREDIENTS

3 medium potatoes, peeled and cut into chunks

2 tbsp reduced fat baking spread

2 tbsp plain (all-purpose) flour

600 ml / 1 pint / 2 ½ cups skimmed milk

1 tbsp Dijon mustard

100 g / 3 ½ oz / 1 cup reduced fat Cheddar, grated

1 small broccoli, broken into florets

250 g / 9 oz / 1 ⅔ cups skinless boneless cod, cut into large chunks

METHOD

1. Boil the potatoes in salted water for 10 minutes, then drain well.

2. Meanwhile, put the baking spread, flour and milk in a saucepan.

3. Stir over a medium heat until it bubbles and thickens, then stir in the cheddar. Season with salt and pepper to taste.

4. Mix the potatoes with the broccoli and cod in a flan dish that will fit snugly inside your slow cooker and top with the sauce.

5. Make a cross from strips of foil inside the slow cooker to help you remove the flan dish, then lower it in. Cover and cook on medium for 3 hours or until the broccoli is tender to the point of a knife.

6. Remove the flan dish from the slow cooker and brown the top under a hot grill for a few minutes before serving.

Risotto baked pumpkins

SERVES: 2 | PREP TIME: 30 MINUTES | COOKING TIME: 5 HOURS

INGREDIENTS

1 litre / 1 pint 15 fl. oz / 4 cups vegetable stock

2 tbsp olive oil

1 onion, finely chopped

1 carrot, finely chopped

2 cloves of garlic, crushed

4 thick rashers bacon, chopped

150 g / 5 ½ oz / ¾ cup risotto rice

50 g / 1 ¾ oz / ½ cup Parmesan, finely grated

2 small culinary pumpkins, tops sliced off and seeds removed

METHOD

1. Heat the stock in a saucepan and keep it just below simmering point.

2. Heat the olive oil in a sauté pan and gently fry the onion and carrot for 5 minutes without colouring. Add the garlic and bacon and cook for 5 more minutes or until golden, then stir in the rice.

3. When it is well coated with the oil, add half of the stock and cook for 8 minutes, stirring occasionally. Stir in the rest of the stock and cook for 5 minutes, then stir in the Parmesan.

4. Arrange the pumpkins side by side in a large oval slow cooker and fill with the par-cooked risotto, then put the tops back on.

5. Pour enough boiling water into the slow cooker to come half way up the sides of the pumpkins, then cover and cook on high for 5 hours or until a skewer slides easily into the pumpkins.

Braised beef with oyster sauce

SERVES: 4 | PREP TIME: 10 MINUTES | COOKING TIME: 6 HOURS

INGREDIENTS

2 tbsp sunflower oil

450 g / 1 lb / 3 cups shin of beef, cut into large chunks

3 cloves of garlic, peeled and squashed

30 g / 1 oz piece of fresh root ginger, sliced

4 spring onions (scallions), green part sliced, the rest bruised

75 ml / 2 ½ fl. oz / ⅓ cup shaoxing rice wine

75 ml / 2 ½ fl. oz / ⅓ cup oyster sauce

2 tbsp dark soy sauce

steamed rice, to serve

1 handful coriander (cilantro) leaves

METHOD

1. Heat the oil in a frying pan and sear the beef on all sides. Transfer the beef to a slow cooker and add the garlic, ginger, spring onion whites, rice wine, oyster sauce and soy sauce.

2. Add enough cold water to just cover the beef, then cover and cook on low for 6 hours.

3. Strain the cooking liquor into a wide saucepan and reduce over a high heat until just thick enough to coat the beef.

4. Serve the beef on a bed of steamed rice with the sauce spooned over. Garnish with coriander leaves and spring onion greens.

Sausage and lentil stew

SERVES: 4 | PREP TIME: 10 MINUTES | COOKING TIME: 3 HOURS

INGREDIENTS

2 tbsp olive oil

16 small sausages

1 onion, sliced

1 stick celery, sliced

1 red pepper, deseeded and diced

2 cloves of garlic, sliced

200 g / 7 oz / 1 cup green lentils

400 g / 14 oz / 2 cups canned tomatoes, chopped

1 bay leaf

1 large handful flat leaf parsley

METHOD

1. Heat the oil in a large frying pan and brown the sausages all over.

2. Transfer to a slow cooker and stir in the rest of the ingredients, except for the parsley. Fill up the tomato can with water and stir it in.

3. Cover and cook on medium for 3 hours.

4. Taste the stew for seasoning and adjust with salt and pepper, then discard the bay leaf and stir in the parsley.

5. Ladle into warm bowls and serve.

Slow-roast lamb shanks

SERVES: 4-6 | PREP TIME: 10 MINUTES | COOKING TIME: 4 HOURS

INGREDIENTS

3 lamb shanks

2 tbsp olive oil

2 tbsp thyme, chopped

2 tbsp rosemary, chopped

2 tbsp oregano, chopped

6 cloves of garlic

300 ml / 10 fl. oz / 1 ¼ cup reduced salt
vegetable stock

METHOD

1. Preheat the oven to 220°C (200°C fan) / 425F /
   gas 7. Rub the land shanks with the oil and
   season with salt and black pepper.

2. Roll the meat in the chopped herbs and place
   into a roasting tray. Scatter with the garlic
   and pour the stock into the pan.

3. Place the lamb into the oven and roast for
   20 minutes.

4. Turn the heat down to 140°C (120°C fan) /
   275F / gas 1 and cover the lamb with foil.
   Roast for a further 3 ½ hours or until the
   meat is falling from the bone.

Thick beef stew

SERVES: 6 | PREP TIME: 30 MINUTES | COOKING TIME: 5 HOURS

INGREDIENTS

low calorie cooking spray
1 onion, diced
2 cloves of garlic, minced
4 carrots, diced
2 sticks of celery, chopped
800 g / 1 lb 12 oz lean beef, diced
1 tbsp plain (all purpose) flour
4 large potatoes, peeled and sliced
4 turnips, diced
4 sprigs of thyme
2 bay leaves
750 ml / 25 fl. oz / 3 cups reduced salt beef stock
250 ml / 9 fl. oz / 1 cup reduced fat cream
1 tbsp cornflour (cornstarch)

METHOD

1. Heat the cooking spray in a frying pan over a medium heat. Add the onions and cook for 4-5 minutes. Add the garlic, carrots and celery and cook for a further minute.

2. Add the beef and brown in the pan for 2-3 minutes. Stir through the flour.

3. Transfer to a slow cooker. Add the potatoes, turnips, thyme, bay leaves and stock. Set on low and cook for 5 hours. Stir in the cream. Dissolve the cornflour in some water to form a paste and stir through. Cook for a further hour. Season before serving.

Roast lamb with vegetables

SERVES: 4 | PREP TIME: 20 MINUTES | COOKING TIME: 6 HOURS

INGREDIENTS

1 kg / 2 lb 3 oz leg of lamb, boneless and rolled

1 bulb of garlic

1 bunch of rosemary

250 ml / 9 fl. oz / 1 cup low salt lamb stock

1 red onion, cut into wedges

4 carrots, roughly sliced

2 sticks of celery, sliced

METHOD

1. Preheat the oven to 140°C (120°C fan) / 275F / gas 1. Place the lamb into a roasting dish and make several holes in the flesh with a knife. Place a clove of garlic and some rosemary leaves into each hole. Scatter the remaining garlic and herbs around the meat. Season.

2. Cover tightly with foil and roast in the oven for up to 4 hours.

3. Scatter the onion, carrots and celery around the meat and return to the oven and roast for a further 2 hours uncovered. Remove from the oven, cover and allow to rest for 20 minutes before carving.

4. Serve with traditional trimmings.

Beef and vegetable stew

SERVES: 4 | PREP TIME: 15 MINUTES | COOKING TIME: 6 HOURS

INGREDIENTS

450 g / 1 lb / 3 cups beef shin, cut into large chunks

2 tbsp plain (all-purpose) flour

2 tbsp olive oil

4 large shallots, halved

2 medium carrots, cut into chunks

8 new potatoes, peeled and quartered

2 cloves of garlic, sliced

150 ml / 5 ½ fl. oz / ⅔ cup red wine

750 ml / 1 pint 5 ½ fl. oz / 3 cups beef stock

2 bay leaves

METHOD

1. Season the beef with salt and pepper and dust the pieces with flour to coat. Heat the oil in a large frying pan and sear the beef in batches on all sides.

2. Transfer the beef to a slow cooker and add the rest of the ingredients.

3. Cover and cook on low for 6 hours, stirring every 2 hours. Season to taste with salt and pepper before serving.

69

Mini quiches

SERVES: 6 | PREP TIME: 45 MINUTES | COOKING TIME: 2 HOURS 50 MINUTES

INGREDIENTS

2 tbsp olive oil

1 small onion, finely chopped

2 thick rashers smoked streaky bacon, chopped

1 clove of garlic, finely chopped

3 large eggs

200 ml / 7 fl. oz / ¾ cup skimmed milk

100 g / 3 ½ oz / 1 cup reduced fat Cheddar, grated

FOR THE PASTRY

100 g / 3 ½ oz / ½ cup reduced fat baking spread, cubed

200 g / 7 oz / 1 ⅓ cups plain (all-purpose) flour

1 large egg, beaten

METHOD

1. To make the pastry, rub the baking spread into the flour until the mixture resembles fine breadcrumbs. Stir in enough cold water to bring the pastry together into a pliable dough and chill for 30 minutes.

2. Meanwhile, heat the oil in a frying pan and fry the onion for 5 minutes. Add the bacon and garlic and cook for another 5 minutes.

3. Gently whisk the eggs with the milk until smoothly combined then stir in the bacon mixture and two thirds of the cheese. Season generously with salt and pepper.

4. Roll out the pastry on a floured surface and cut out six circles with a cookie cutter. Transfer the pastry circles to a six-hole cupcake tin that will fit inside your slow cooker.

5. Cover the slow cooker with a clean tea towel, then put on the lid. Cook on high for 1 hour.

6. Pour the filling into the pastry cases and sprinkle with the rest of the cheese, then cover with the tea towel and lid and cook on low for 1 hour, 30 minutes.

Ragu for pasta

SERVES: 4 | PREP TIME: 20 MINUTES | COOKING TIME: 5 HOURS

INGREDIENTS

2 tbsp olive oil

1 onion, finely chopped

1 large carrot, diced

1 stick celery, diced

1 tbsp fresh thyme leaves

4 cloves of garlic, finely chopped

450 g / 1 lb / 3 cups shin of beef, cubed

2 tbsp concentrated tomato puree

200 ml / 7 fl. oz / ¾ cup red wine

400 ml / 14 fl. oz / 1 ½ cups beef stock

2 tbsp flat leaf parsley, chopped

tagliatelle to serve

METHOD

1. Heat the oil in a large frying pan and fry the onion, carrot, celery and thyme for 10 minutes, stirring occasionally. Add the garlic and beef and fry until the meat starts to brown then stir in the tomato puree.

2. Pour in the wine and boil rapidly for 2 minutes, then scrape everything into a slow cooker with the beef stock. Cover the slow cooker and cook on medium for 5 hours, then season. The meat should be falling apart into shreds by this time.

3. Stir in the parsley and serve with freshly cooked tagliatelle.

Rich braised lamb shanks

SERVES: 4 | PREP TIME: 25 MINUTES | COOKING TIME: 8 HOURS

INGREDIENTS

2 tbsp olive oil

1 onion, quartered and sliced

2 cloves of garlic, finely chopped

4 lamb shanks

2 tbsp plain (all-purpose) flour

4 carrots, peeled and cut into batons

400 ml / 14 fl. oz / 1 ⅔ cups port

400 ml / 14 fl. oz / 1 ⅔ cups lamb or beef stock

1 sprig of rosemary

METHOD

1. Heat the oil in a frying pan and fry the onion and garlic for 10 minutes or until soft and golden. Season with salt and pepper, then tip it into a slow cooker.

2. Dust the lamb shanks with flour, then sear them all over in the frying pan. Sit the lamb on top of the onions and surround with the carrots.

3. Pour the port into the frying pan and boil for 5 minutes, then pour it into the slow cooker with the stock and rosemary.

4. Cook on high for 8 hours or until the lamb is tender and the sauce is thick and rich. Taste and adjust the seasoning before serving.

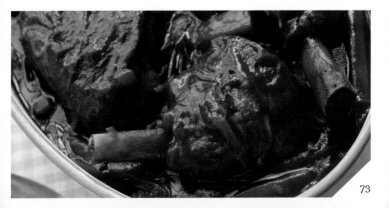

73

Chorizo and butterbean stew

SERVES: 6 | PREP TIME: 15 MINUTES | COOKING TIME: 7 HOURS

INGREDIENTS

300 g / 10 ½ oz / 2 cups dried butterbeans, soaked overnight

4 cooking chorizo, sliced

1 onion, chopped

2 small carrots, sliced

1 stick celery, sliced

2 cloves of garlic, sliced

1 bay leaf

150 g / 5 ½ oz / 1 cup sundried tomatoes

750 ml / 1 pint 5 ½ fl. oz / 3 cups chicken stock

TO SERVE

250 g / 9 oz / 2 balls mozzarella, torn into small chunks

1 small bunch flat leaf parsley, chopped

1 small bunch dill, chopped

METHOD

1. Drain the beans of their soaking water, then tip them into a saucepan, cover with cold water and bring to the boil. Cook for 10 minutes then drain well.

2. Meanwhile, cook the chorizo slices in a hot frying pan until coloured on both sides.

3. Tip the beans and chorizo into a slow cooker and stir in the rest of the ingredients. Cover and cook on medium for 7 hours or until the beans are tender. Season to taste with salt and pepper.

4. Divide the stew between six warm bowls and arrange the mozzarella, parsley and dill on top.

Mini toad in the holes with gravy

SERVES: 12 | PREP TIME: 10 MINUTES | COOKING TIME: 5 HOURS 15 MINUTES

INGREDIENTS

2 tbsp olive oil

2 onions, halved and sliced

1 tbsp balsamic vinegar

1 tbsp runny honey

1 tbsp plain (all-purpose) flour

50 ml / 1 ¾ fl. oz / ¼ cup dry Marsala

500 ml / 17 ½ fl. oz / 2 cups chicken stock

2 tbsp lard

6 good quality sausages, halved

75 g / 2 ½ oz / ½ cup plain (all-purpose) flour

2 large eggs

100 ml / 3 ½ fl. oz / ½ cup skimmed milk

rosemary sprigs, to garnish

METHOD

1. Heat the oil in a slow cooker on high for 15 minutes. Stir in the onions, balsamic and honey. Cover and cook on high for 1 hour, stirring every 15 minutes.

2. Stir in the flour, then gradually incorporate the Marsala and stock. Cover and cook on low for 4 hours, stirring occasionally.

3. An hour before you want to serve, preheat the oven to 230°C (210°C fan) / 450F / gas 8. Heat 1 teaspoon of lard in a frying pan and brown the sausages all over.

4. Put a blob of lard into each hole of a 12-hole muffin tin. Put in the oven to heat.

5. Put the flour in a large jug with a pinch of salt, then whisk in the eggs and milk.

6. Take the muffin tin out of the oven, add a sausage half to each hole and divide the batter between them. Return the tin to the oven and bake for 35 minutes without opening the door. Serve the toads with onion gravy and rosemary to garnish.

Cheesy chicken bake

SERVES: 4 | PREP TIME: 15 MINUTES | COOKING TIME: 3 HOURS

INGREDIENTS

1 large aubergine, thinly sliced

150 ml / 5 ½ fl. oz / ⅔ cup dry white wine

3 skinless chicken breasts, sliced

225 g / 8 oz / 1 ½ cups cherry tomatoes, halved

125 g / 4 ½ oz / 1 ball light mozzarella, grated

100 g / 3 ½ oz / 1 cup reduced fat Cheddar, grated

100 g / 3 ½ oz / ½ cup low fat soft cheese

1 tsp herbs de Provence

1 clove of garlic, crushed

METHOD

1. Arrange the aubergine slices in a slow cooker and season with salt and pepper. Pour over the wine, then top with the chicken and tomatoes.

2. Mix the mozzarella, Cheddar, soft cheese, herbs and garlic together and dot the mixture over the top.

3. Cover and cook on medium for 3 hours or until the chicken is cooked through.

4. If you prefer, the top can be coloured under a hot grill just before serving.

Garlic baked chicken

SERVES: 6 | PREP TIME: 10 MINUTES | COOKING TIME: 3 HOURS

INGREDIENTS

1 chicken, jointed into 12 pieces

1 bulb of garlic, separated into cloves

1 lemon, juiced

2 tbsp Stevia

75 ml / 2 ½ fl. oz / ⅓ cup reduced sodium soy sauce

METHOD

1. Mix all of the ingredients together in a slow cooker and season with black pepper.

2. Cover and cook on medium for 3 hours, stirring once an hour.

3. Transfer everything to a baking dish and brown under a hot grill for a few minutes to finish.

Lamb hotpot

SERVES: 6 | PREP TIME: 25 MINUTES | COOKING TIME: 3 HOURS

INGREDIENTS

1 kg / 2 lb 3 ½ oz / 7 cups boneless lamb neck, cubed

3 lamb kidneys, trimmed and quartered

2 tbsp olive oil

1 onion, chopped

2 carrots, peeled and cut into chunks

2 sticks celery, cut into chunks

6 sprigs fresh thyme

1 tbsp plain (all-purpose) flour

800 ml / 1 pint 7 fl. oz / 3 ¼ cups lamb or chicken stock

1 kg / 2 lb 3 ½ oz potatoes

METHOD

1. Preheat the oven to 160°C (140° fan) / 325F / gas 3.

2. Blot the lamb and kidneys with kitchen paper to ensure they are completely dry then season with salt and pepper. Heat the oil in a frying pan over a high heat then sear the lamb and kidneys in batches until browned all over.

3. Remove the meat from the pan, lower the heat a little and add the onions, carrots, celery and thyme. Cook for 10 minutes, stirring occasionally.

4. Increase the heat and stir in the flour then incorporate the stock and bring to a simmer. Arrange the lamb and kidneys in a casserole dish and pour over the stock and vegetables.

5. Slice the potatoes 5 mm (¼ in) thick with a sharp knife or mandolin and arrange them on top of the lamb.

6. Cover the dish tightly with foil or a lid. Bake for 2 hours 30 minutes, then remove the foil and bake for another 30 minutes to colour the top.

81

Shepherd's pie

SERVES: 6 | PREP TIME: 30 MINUTES | COOKING TIME: 5 HOURS

INGREDIENTS

2 tbsp olive oil

2 large onion, finely chopped

2 cloves of garlic, crushed

2 tsp fresh rosemary, finely chopped

450 g / 1 lb / 2 cups lean minced lamb

500 ml / 17 ½ fl. oz / 2 cups lamb or beef stock

1 tsp Worcestershire sauce

2 tsp redcurrant jelly

2 tsp fresh mint, finely chopped

FOR THE TOPPING

450 g / 1 lb floury potatoes, peeled and cubed

150 ml / 5 ½ fl. oz / ⅔ cup skimmed milk

50 g / 1 ¾ oz / ⅔ cup fresh breadcrumbs

50 g / 1 ¾ oz / ½ cup reduced fat Cheddar, grated

METHOD

1. Heat the oil in a large frying pan and fry the onions for 10 minutes, stirring occasionally. Add the garlic and rosemary and cook for 2 minutes, then add the mince.

2. Fry the mince until it starts to brown then scrape the mixture into a slow cooker and add the stock, Worcester sauce and redcurrant jelly.

3. Cover the slow cooker and cook on medium for 5 hours.

4. Towards the end of the cooking time, cook the potatoes in salted water for 12 minutes, or until they are tender, then drain well. Return the potatoes to the saucepan and add the milk, then mash until smooth.

5. Stir the mint into the cooked mince and season to taste with salt and pepper. Transfer it to an ovenproof frying pan and top with mashed potatoes.

6. Mix the breadcrumbs with the cheese and scatter over the top, then cook under a hot grill for a few minutes or until golden brown.

Chicken and sweet potato stew

SERVES: 2-4 | PREP TIME: **20 MINUTES** | COOKING TIME: **1 HOUR**

INGREDIENTS

!ow calorie cooking spray

1 onion, diced

2 cloves of garlic, minced

400 g / 14 oz chicken breast

1 tsp paprika

1 tsp cayenne

2 tsp thyme leaves

1 tsp tomato puree

500 ml / 17 fl. oz / 2 cups low salt vegetable stock

300 g / 10 ½ oz sweet potatoes, peeled and diced

200 g / 7 oz kale, chopped

METHOD

1. Preheat the oven to 180°C (160°C fan) / 350F / gas 4.

2. Heat some cooking spray in a frying pan or skillet. Add the onions and cook for 4-5 minutes until softened. Add the garlic and cook for a further 1-2 minutes until fragrant.

3. Add the chicken, paprika, cayenne, thyme and tomato puree. Fry for 3-4 minutes.

4. Transfer to an ovenproof dish. Pour over the stock and add the sweet potatoes. Cover and bake in the oven for up to 1 hour, removing once or twice to mix the ingredients.

5. Place the kale into a pan of boiling water and cook for 4-5 minutes until tender. Drain and mix into the chicken and sweet potatoes. Season to taste before serving.

84

Pulled pork pasties

SERVES: 4-6 | PREP TIME: 20 MINUTES | COOKING TIME: 6 HOURS

INGREDIENTS

800 g / 1 lb 12 oz pork loin joint

1 tbsp smoked paprika

1 tbsp cayenne

1 tbsp garlic powder

1 tsp chilli (chili) flakes

400 g / 14 oz canned chopped tomatoes

50 g / 1 ¾ oz unsweetened apple sauce

2 tbsp fruit syrup

2 tbsp whole wheat flour

300 g / 10 ½ oz puff pastry

1 egg beaten

METHOD

1. Rub the pork all over with the paprika, cayenne, garlic and chilli flakes. Cook in a slow cooker with the tomatoes, apple sauce and fruit syrup on low for 5 - 6 hours.

2. Remove the pork from the slow cooker and pull apart with forks. Whisk the flour into the sauce to thicken before returning the meat to the sauce. Season and leave to cool.

3. Preheat the oven to 180°C (160°C fan) / 350F / gas 4 and line a baking tray with greaseproof paper. Roll out the pastry and cut out circles to the desired size for your pasties. Spoon the filling into the centre of the pastry circles before folding and sealing the edges.

4. Make a small hole in the pasties and brush with the beaten egg before baking in the oven for 20 minutes until golden brown.

Paella with chorizo

SERVES: 4-5 | PREP TIME: 20 MINUTES | COOKING TIME: 3 HOURS, 30 MINUTES

INGREDIENTS

1 tbsp olive oil

1 onion, diced

2 red peppers, sliced

2 cloves of garlic

400 g / 14 oz chicken breast, sliced

1 tsp smoked paprika

pinch of saffron

500 g / 1 lb 1 oz / 2 ½ cups paella rice

1 l / 33 ¾ fl. oz / 4 cups reduced salt chicken stock, hot

1 chorizo sausage, sliced

METHOD

1. Heat the oil in frying pan. Add the onion and peppers and fry for 2-3 minutes until softened. Add the garlic and paprika and fry for a further minute. Add the chicken and cook for a further 2-3 minutes to colour.

2. Stir in the saffron and rice, mixing through the onions to coat in the oil. Transfer to a slow cooker and pour over the stock. Set to high and cook for 3 hours. Turn off and leave to stand for 20 minutes.

3. Heat a griddle pan until smoking and add the chorizo. Cook for 5-6 minutes until charred. Serve the paella topped with the grilled sausage.

Lamb chops

SERVES: 4 | PREP TIME: 30 MINUTES | COOKING TIME: 2 HOURS

INGREDIENTS

2 tbsp olive oil

16 small lamb chops

100 ml / 3 ½ fl. oz / ½ cup dry white wine

1 onion, finely chopped

2 cloves of garlic, crushed

400 ml / 7 fl. oz / 1 ⅔ cups tomato passata

2 tsp dried mint

400 g / 14 oz linguini

METHOD

1. Heat the oil in a frying pan and sear the lamb chops on both sides.

2. Transfer the lamb to a slow cooker and add the wine to the frying pan. Simmer for 2 minutes, then pour into the slow cooker and add the onion, garlic and passata. Cover and cook on high for 2 hours.

3. Boil the linguini in salted water according to the packet instructions. Drain well.

4. Meanwhile, remove the lamb from the slow cooker and scrape most of the sauce back into the pot. Sprinkle with dried mint and cook under a hot grill for a few minutes on each side to caramelize the sauce.

5. Stir the linguini into the tomato sauce and serve with the lamb chops.

Roast beef rib

SERVES: 6 | PREP TIME: 30 MINUTES | MARINATE: 2 HOURS | COOKING TIME: 6 HOURS

INGREDIENTS

1 tbsp fresh rosemary, finely chopped

1 tbsp fresh thyme leaves

2 cloves of garlic, crushed

2 tbsp olive oil

1.8 kg / 4 lb rib of beef, on the bone

2 onions, sliced

250 ml / 9 fl. oz / 1 cup red wine

250 ml / 9 fl. oz / 1 cup beef stock

1 tbsp plain (all-purpose) flour, optional

METHOD

1. Mix the rosemary, thyme and garlic and rub it all over the beef. Season all over with salt and pepper, then leave to marinate at room temperature for 2 hours.

2. Heat the oil in a large frying pan and sear the beef all over until well browned.

3. Arrange the onions in an even layer in a slow cooker and sit the beef on top. Pour in the wine and stock.

4. Cover and cook on low for 6 hours or until it reaches an internal temperature of 54°C (130F) when checked with a probe thermometer.

5. Transfer the meat to a carving board and cover with a double layer of foil. Leave to rest for 15 minutes.

6. Meanwhile, strain the cooking liquor into a saucepan and bring to the boil. Reduce the liquid until it tastes suitably flavoursome. It can then be thickened by whisking in a little flour if you prefer.

7. Carve the beef into thick slices and serve the gravy on the side.

Raised pork pie

SERVES: 3 | PREP TIME: 30 MINUTES | COOKING TIME: 3 HOURS, 30 MINUTES

INGREDIENTS

50 g / 1 ¾ oz / ¼ cup reduced fat baking spread

200 g / 7 oz / 1 ⅓ cups plain (all-purpose) flour

50 g / 1 ¾ oz / ⅓ cup strong white bread flour

50 g / 1 ¾ oz / ¼ cup lard

200 g / 7 oz / 1 ⅓ cups lean minced pork

200 g / 7 oz / 1 ⅓ cups pork loin, finely chopped

100 g / 3 ½ oz / ⅔ cup smoked streaky bacon,
finely chopped

1 onion, finely grated

1 tsp fresh sage, finely chopped

½ tsp white peppercorns, freshly ground

½ tsp nutmeg, freshly grated

METHOD

1. Rub the butter into the two flours with 1
    teaspoon of salt until the mixture resembles
    fine breadcrumbs.

2. Put the lard in a saucepan with 100 ml water
    and bring to the boil, then stir it into
    the flour.

3. Turn out the dough and knead for 1 minute
    or until smooth. Reserve a quarter of the
    dough for making the lid then roll the rest
    out into a large circle and use it to line the
    base and 10 cm (4 in) up the sides of a small
    slow cooker.

4. Mix the rest of the ingredients together and
    season with salt. Pack the mixture
    into the pastry case and brush round the
    outside with water. Roll out the reserved
    pastry for the lid and crimp the edges. Trim
    away any excess pastry and slash a
    hole in the top for the steam to escape.

5. Chill the slow cooker insert for 30 minutes to
    firm up the pastry, then reassemble and cook
    on high for 1 hour 30 minutes.

6. Reduce the temperature to low and cook for
    5 hours or until an internal temperature
    probe reads 72°C (160F). Leave to cool
    completely before cutting and serving.

Chicken and ham bake

SERVES: 4-6 | PREP TIME: 20 MINUTES | COOKING TIME: 1 HOUR, 15 MINUTES

INGREDIENTS

4 large potatoes, peeled and sliced

low calories cooking spray

2 leeks, sliced

2 cloves of garlic, minced

50 g / 1 ¾ oz / ⅓ cup plain (all purpose) flour

1 tsp white pepper

1 tsp paprika

300 ml / 10 fl. oz / 1 ¼ cup skimmed milk

150 ml / 5 ¼ fl. oz / ⅔ cup reduced fat double (heavy) cream

1 tbsp Dijon mustard

500 g / 1 lb 1 oz cooked chicken, shredded

150 g / 5 ¼ oz cooked ham, diced

200 g / 7 oz / 2 cups low fat Cheddar cheese, grated

200 g / 7 oz / 1 ⅓ cups panko breadcrumbs

METHOD

1. Preheat the oven to 180°C (160°C fan) / 350F / gas 4.

2. Place the potato slices into a pan of boiling water. Cook for 8-10 minutes until softened but still firm, drain and set aside.

3. Spray some oil into a heavy bottomed pan over a medium heat. Add the leeks and cook for 5-6 minutes until softened. Add the garlic and cook for a further 1-2 minutes.

4. Stir the flour, pepper and paprika into the leeks before adding the milk and cream. Continue to cook, stirring continuously, until the sauce has thickened. Mix the mustard, chicken and ham into the sauce.

5. Pour the chicken and ham filling into a suitably sized ovenproof dish. Top with the potato slices, cheese and breadcrumbs before placing into the oven and cooking for 1 hour.

6. Remove and serve immediately.

Beef stroganoff

SERVES: 4 | PREP TIME: 20 MINUTES | COOKING TIME: 6 HOURS

INGREDIENTS

2 tbsp olive oil

450 g / 1 lb braising steak, sliced

1 large onion, chopped

150 g / 5 ½ oz / 2 cups button mushrooms, sliced

1 tsp Hungarian paprika

250 ml / 9 fl. oz / 1 cup beef stock

250 ml / 9 fl. oz / 1 cup half fat soured cream

1 small bunch flat-leaf parsley, chopped

boiled rice, to serve

METHOD

1. Heat half the oil in a frying pan and sear the steak slices on both sides in batches. Transfer to a slow cooker.

2. Add the rest of the oil to the pan and fry the onions over a medium heat for 10 minutes to soften. Scrape the onions into the slow cooker and add the mushrooms, paprika and stock.

3. Cover the cook on low for 4 hours.

4. Stir in the soured cream and season to taste with salt and pepper.

5. Cover and cook for 2 hours or until the beef is tender.

6. Sprinkle the stroganoff with parsley and serve with boiled rice.

Asian braised beef

SERVES: 4 | PREP TIME: 20 MINUTES | COOKING TIME: 6 HOURS

INGREDIENTS

2 tbsp sunflower oil

450 g / 1 lb / 3 cups chuck steak, cut into
large chunks

30 g / 1 oz piece of fresh root ginger, sliced

4 spring onions (scallions), green part sliced,
the rest bruised

1 bulb of garlic, halved horizontally

1 small bunch coriander (cilantro),
leaves separated from stems

2 kaffir lime leaves

75 ml / 2 ½ fl. oz / ⅓ cup shaoxing rice wine

75 ml / 2 ½ fl. oz / ⅓ cup light soy sauce

300 g / 10 ½ oz thin egg noodles

½ Chinese cabbage, quartered

150 g / 5 ½ oz / 2 cups shimeji mushrooms

2 hot red chillies (chilies), sliced

1 lime, cut into wedges

METHOD

1. Heat the oil in a frying pan and sear the beef
   on all sides. Transfer the beef to a slow
   cooker and add the ginger, bruised spring
   onion whites, garlic, coriander stems, lime
   leaves, rice wine and soy sauce.

2. Add enough cold water to cover the beef,
   then cover and cook on low for 6 hours.

3. Cook the noodles according to the packet
   instructions and drain well. Divide between
   four bowls.

4. Poach the cabbage and mushrooms in 2
   ladles of the beef cooking liquor for
   3 minutes, then divide between the bowls.

5. Ladle in the beef and cooking liquor and
   garnish with coriander leaves,
   spring onion greens and chillies. Serve with
   lime wedges for squeezing over.

Beef pastries

SERVES: 4 | PREP TIME: 20 MINUTES | COOKING TIME: 6 HOURS

INGREDIENTS

2 tbsp olive oil

500 g / 1 lb 1 oz lean beef, diced

1 onion, roughly chopped

1 tbsp flour

4 carrots, diced

750 ml / 25 fl. oz / 3 cups low salt beef stock

4 potatoes, cubed

2 sprigs of thyme

500 g / 1 lb 1 oz puff pastry

1 egg, beaten

METHOD

1. Heat the oil in a heavy bottomed casserole pan over a high heat and add the beef. Cook for 2 minutes to brown the meat before removing with a slotted spoon.

2. Add the onion and carrots to the pan and fry for 3-5 minutes until starting to brown at the edges. Return the beef and any juices that have been collected to the pan and stir through the flour.

3. Add the beef and vegetables to a slow cooker and add the stock, potatoes and thyme. Cook on the low setting for 4-6 hours, until the beef is soft and vegetables are tender. Remove and allow to cool.

4. Preheat the oven to 220°C (200°C fan) / 425F / gas 7 and line a baking tray with greaseproof paper.

5. Roll out the party on a clean dry surface. Cut into four equal sized squares.

6. Spoon the cooled beef and vegetables onto one half of the square in the centre. Brush around the edges of the pastry with egg and fold over to seal the meat within the pastry. Seal the edges and score the tops of the pastries.

7. Place onto the prepared baking tray and brush the tops with egg. Bake in the oven to 25-30 minutes until golden and crisp.

Chicken and vegetable broth

SERVES: 4 | PREP TIME: 10 MINUTES | COOKING TIME: 4 HOURS

INGREDIENTS

3 skinless chicken breasts, cut into chunks

2 carrots, peeled and crinkle cut

2 sticks celery, sliced

3 medium potatoes, peeled and diced

1 head broccoli, broken into florets

1 onion, finely chopped

1 litre / 1 pint 15 fl. oz / 4 cups chicken stock

150 g / 5 ½ oz / 1 cup peas, defrosted if frozen

METHOD

1. Mix all of the ingredients except for the peas in a slow cooker and season with salt and pepper.

2. Cover and cook on medium for 2 hours or until the vegetables are tender and the chicken is cooked.

3. Turn off the heat, then add the peas, cover and leave to stand for 5 minutes.

4. Ladle into four bowls and serve immediately.

Lamb and apricot tagine

SERVES: 4 | PREP TIME: 20 MINUTES | COOKING TIME: 6 HOURS

INGREDIENTS

450 g / 1 lb / 2 cups lamb shoulder, cubed

2 tbsp olive oil

1 onion, finely chopped

1 large carrot, diced

2 cloves of garlic, finely chopped

2 tsp ras el hanout spice mix

100 g / 3 ½ oz / ¾ cup dried chickpeas

600 ml / 1 pint / 2 ½ cups lamb or vegetable stock

150 g / 5 ½ oz / 1 cup dried apricots

½ pomegranate, seeds only

2 tbsp flat leaf parsley, chopped

METHOD

1. Season the lamb all over with salt and pepper. Heat the oil in a frying pan and sear the lamb on all sides, then transfer the pieces to a slow cooker.

2. Fry the onion, carrot and garlic in the frying pan for 5 minutes, then stir in the ras el hanout.

3. Scrape the mixture into the slow cooker and add the chickpeas and stock. Cover and cook on medium for 6 hours, adding the apricots after 4 hours.

4. Season to taste with salt and pepper and ladle into warm bowls. Garnish with pomegranate seeds and parsley.

101

Quiche Lorraine

SERVES: 8 | PREP TIME: 45 MINUTES | COOKING TIME: 3 HOURS 30 MINUTES

INGREDIENTS

110 g / 4 oz / ½ cup reduced fat baking spread, cubed and chilled

225 g / 8 oz / 1 ½ cups plain (all-purpose) flour

2 tbsp olive oil

1 leek, finely chopped

6 rashers streaky bacon, chopped

2 cloves of garlic, finely chopped

4 large eggs, beaten

225 ml / 8 fl. oz / ¾ cup skimmed milk

75 g / 2 ½ oz / ½ cup reduced fat cheese, grated

¼ tsp nutmeg, freshly grated

METHOD

1. To make the pastry, rub the baking spread into the flour until the mixture resembles fine breadcrumbs. Stir in just enough cold water to bring the pastry together into a pliable dough, then chill for 30 minutes.

2. Roll out the pastry and use it to line a round flan dish that will fit inside your slow cooker. Cover and cook on high for 2 hours.

3. Heat the oil in a large sauté pan and sauté the leek and bacon for 8 minutes. Add the garlic and cook for 2 minutes, then set aside.

4. Whisk the eggs with the milk then stir in the bacon mixture and cheese. Season generously with salt, pepper and nutmeg.

5. Pour the filling into the pastry case, then cover and cook on low for 1 hour 30 minutes or until the quiche is set in the centre.

6. For a golden finish, colour the top under a hot grill for a few minutes.

Beef bourguignon

SERVES: 6 | PREP TIME: 30 MINUTES | COOKING TIME: 5 HOURS

INGREDIENTS

low calorie cooking spray

500 g / 1 lb 1 oz lean diced beef

1 onion, diced

1 tbsp plain (all purpose) flour

3 cloves of garlic, chopped

2 carrots, diced

1 tbsp tomato puree

250 ml / 9 fl. oz / 1 cup red wine

500 ml / 17 fl. oz / 2 cups low salt beef stock

handful of thyme sprigs

2 bay leaves

50 g / 1 ¾ oz diced bacon, fat removed

200 g / 7 oz chestnut mushrooms, quartered

METHOD

1. Preheat the oven to 160°C (140°C fan) / 325F / gas 3.

2. Spray a large ovenproof casserole dish with cooking oil and place onto a moderately high heat. Brown the meat in batches, remove from the pan with a slotted spoon.

3. Add the onions to the pan and cook for 3-4 minutes until soft and translucent. Return the meat to the pan and add the flour to absorb any juices.

4. Add the garlic, carrots and tomato puree. Mix through the other ingredients for a minute until fragrant.

5. Pour the wine into the pan and leave to cook and bubble for 2-3 minutes. Pour in the stock and add the thyme and bay leaves to the pan. Heat until boiling before placing the lid on the pan and placing into the oven for up to 2 hours.

6. Place a frying pan onto a moderate heat and spray with some oil. Add the bacon and cook for 2-3 minutes until starting to crisp. Add the mushrooms to the pan and cook for a further 3-4 minutes. Add to the casserole and mix through before serving.

7. Season and serve in bowls with crusty bread to soak up the liquid.

Chicken pie filling

SERVES: 4 | PREP TIME: 30 MINUTES | COOKING TIME: 4 HOURS, 45 MINUTES

INGREDIENTS

4 chicken leg quarters

1 carrot, cut into chunks

1 stick celery, cut into chunks

1 leek, cut into chunks

2 tsp cornflour (corn starch)

1 tsp Dijon mustard

150 ml / 5 ½ fl. oz / ⅔ cup 0 % fat Greek yogurt

1 courgette (zucchini), chopped

FOR THE PASTRY

200 g / 7 oz / 1 cup reduced fat baking spread, cubed and chilled

400 g / 14 oz / 2 ⅔ cups plain (all-purpose) flour

1 egg, beaten

METHOD

1. Put the chicken, carrot, celery and leek in a slow cooker and add enough water to cover. Cover and cook on medium for 4 hours.

2. Strain and reserve the stock. Discard the vegetables, chicken skin and bones then shred the chicken into pieces. Stir the cornflour and mustard into the yogurt then stir in the chicken and enough of the stock to make a thin sauce. Leave to cool.

3. While the filling is cooking, rub the butter into the flour until the mixture resembles breadcrumbs. Stir in water to bring the pastry into a dough. Chill for 30 minutes.

4. Preheat the oven to 200°C (180° fan) / 400F / gas 6. Roll out ⅔ of the pastry on a floured surface and use it to line a pie dish. Spoon in the filling then brush round the rim with water. Roll out the rest of the pastry and lay it over the top. Trim away any excess. Crimp round the edge with a fork and brush the top with beaten egg. Make a few steam holes on top with a sharp knife.

5. Bake the pie for 45 minutes.

Malaysian beef curry

SERVES: 4-6 | PREP TIME: 20 MINUTES | COOKING TIME: 3 HOURS

INGREDIENTS

4 birds eye chillies (chili)

2 cloves of garlic

25 g / 1 oz ginger, peeled

1 tsp paprika

1 tsp turmeric

½ tsp cloves, ground

½ tsp cinnamon

½ tsp nutmeg ground

2 tbsp coconut oil

800 g 1 lb 12 oz lean diced beef

2 onions, sliced

2 red peppers, sliced

2 sticks of lemongrass

1 cinnamon stick

400 ml / 13 ½ fl. oz / 1 ⅔ cups low fat coconut milk

500 ml / 17 fl. oz / 2 cups reduced salt beef stock

4 spring onions (scallions), sliced

300 g / 10 ½ oz / 1 ½ cups rice, cooked

METHOD

1. Preheat the oven to 150°C (130°C fan) / 300F / gas 2.

2. Place the first eight ingredients into a blender along with half the coconut oil and pulse to form a curry paste. Mix the beef with the paste to coat.

3. Heat the remaining oil in a large casserole with a lid. Add the onions and peppers and cook for 4-5 minutes until softened.

4. Add the beef and cook for 4-5 minutes until fragrant and browned. Add the lemongrass and cinnamon to the pan before pouring in the coconut milk and stock.

5. Heat until boiling, stirring to combine all the ingredients. Once boiling, cover and place into the oven for around 3 hours until the meat is tender.

6. Mix through the spring onions and serve with the cooked rice.

Asian beef with noodles

SERVES: 2 | PREP TIME: 20 MINUTES | COOKING TIME: 3 HOURS, 30 MINUTES

INGREDIENTS

800 g / 1 lb 12 oz rump steak

50 ml / 1 ¾ fl. oz / ¼ cup soy sauce

1" piece of root ginger, sliced

2 cloves of garlic, sliced

2 tbsp sesame oil

1 tbsp honey

1 tbsp rice wine vinegar

1 tsp Chinese five spice

400 g / 14 oz egg noodles

1 red pepper, thinly sliced

300 g / 10 ½ oz green (string) beans, trimmed

METHOD

1. Trim the fat from the steak and slice into smaller pieces. Combine the soy, ginger, garlic, 1 tbsp sesame oil, honey, vinegar and five spice. Mix through the beef and toss to coat. Place into a slow cooker and cook on high for 3 hours. Turn off and leave to stand for 20 minutes.

2. Cook the noodles as per the packet instructions, drain and set aside.

3. Heat the remaining oil in a wok or frying pan over a medium heat. Add the peppers and beans and stir fry for 3-4 minutes.

4. Add the noodles and beef, including the juices from the slow cooked, and toss through the vegetables to combine.

Chilli con carne

SERVES: 4 | PREP TIME: 15 MINUTES | COOKING TIME: 6 HOURS

INGREDIENTS

1 tbsp olive oil

1 red onion, diced

1 red pepper, diced

500 g / 1 lb 1 oz lean beef mince

1 tsp chilli (chili) powder

1 tsp smoked paprika

1 tsp ground cumin

1 tsp ground coriander (cilantro)

400 g / 14 oz tinned chopped tomatoes

200 ml / 7 fl. oz / ¾ cup water

400 g / 14 oz tinned kidney beans, drained

200 g / 7 oz sweetcorn

handful of fresh coriander (cilantro), chopped

METHOD

1. Heat the oil over a medium high heat in a large casserole. Add the onion and pepper and cook for 6-8 minutes until softened.

2. Add the beef mince and brown before adding the chilli powder, paprika, cumin and coriander. Fry for a further minute until fragrant. Add the chopped tomatoes and water, heat until boiling.

3. Transfer to a slow cooker on low and cook for up to 6 hours. Add the kidney beans and sweetcorn after 3 hours.

4. Serve in a bowl with the chopped coriander as a garnish.

Chicken and sweet potato curry

SERVES: 2-4 | PREP TIME: 15 MINUTES | COOKING TIME: 1 HOUR

INGREDIENTS

low calorie cooking spray

1 onion, diced

2 yellow peppers, sliced

2 cloves of garlic, minced

1 chilli (chili), sliced

400 g / 14 oz chicken breast

1 tsp turmeric

1 tsp cumin

1 tsp coriander (cilantro)

1 tsp tomato puree

500 ml / 17 fl. oz / 2 cups low salt chicken stock

300 g / 10 ½ oz sweet potatoes, peeled and diced

METHOD

1. Preheat the oven to 180°C (160°C fan) / 350F / gas 4.

2. Heat some cooking spray in a frying pan or skillet. Add the onions and peppers and cook for 4-5 minutes until softened. Add the garlic and chilli cook for a further 1-2 minutes until fragrant.

3. Add the chicken, turmeric, cumin, coriander and tomato puree. Fry for 3-4 minutes to colour the meat and warm the spices.

4. Transfer the ingredients to an ovenproof dish. Pour over the stock and add the sweet potatoes. Cover and place into the oven and bake for up to 1 hour, removing once or twice to mix the ingredients.

5. Serve with rice or Indian breads as desired.

Lamb pot roast

SERVES: 4-6 | PREP TIME: 15 MINUTES | COOKING TIME: 7 HOURS

INGREDIENTS

800 g / 1 lb 12 oz lamb shoulder

400 ml / 13 ½ fl. oz / 1 ⅔ cups red wine

400 ml / 13 ½ fl. oz / 1 ⅔ cups low salt lamb stock

1 bulb of garlic, halved

2 bay leaves

4 sprigs of thyme

4 sprigs of rosemary

4 carrots, diced

3 leeks, sliced

4 large potatoes, peeled and sliced

small bunch of flat leaf parsley

METHOD

1. Preheat the oven to 220°C (200°C fan) / 425F / gas 7.

2. Season the lamb and place into a large casserole that can accommodate all the ingredients. Place into the oven and roast for 20 minutes. Turn the oven down to 140°C (120°C fan) / 275F / gas 1.

3. Add the wine, stock, garlic, bay leaves, thyme and rosemary to the casserole. Return to the oven and roast for 3 hours.

4. Remove from the oven and skim the fat from the surface of the liquid. Add the vegetables to the pot and roast for a further 3 hours.

5. Remove the meat from the oven to rest before carving. Place the casserole onto the hob and heat to reduce the liquid as desired.

Spanish potatoes with chicken

SERVES: 2-4 | PREP TIME: 15 MINUTES | COOKING TIME: 1 HOUR

INGREDIENTS

500 g / 1 lb 1 oz potatoes, diced

low calorie cooking spray

1 onion, diced

2 cloves of garlic, chopped

300 g / 10 ½ oz chicken breast

2 tsp paprika

1 tbsp tomato purée

50 g / 1 ¾ oz / ¼ cup sundried tomatoes

2 tbsp low fat mayonnaise

METHOD

1. Preheat the oven to 180°C (160°C fan) / 350F / gas 4.

2. Par boil the potatoes for 10 minutes.

3. Spray some oil into a frying pan over a medium heat. Add the onions and cook for 4-5 minutes until softened. Add the garlic and cook for a further minute until fragrant.

4. Add the chicken, paprika and tomato puree and fry for 4-5 minutes to colour the meat.

5. Place the potatoes into an ovenproof dish with the chicken and sundried tomatoes. Toss to combine and season.

6. Roast for 50 minutes. Place into serving bowls before topping with the mayonnaise.

Spicy pulled turkey

SERVES: 8 | PREP TIME: 15 MINUTES | MARINATE: 12 HOURS | COOKING TIME: 6 HOURS

INGREDIENTS

4 skinless turkey thighs, on the bone

2 tbsp barbecue seasoning mix

1 tbsp smoked paprika

2 tbsp olive oil

250 ml / 9 fl. oz / 1 cup chicken stock

2 red chillies (chilies), sliced

potato wedges, to serve

METHOD

1. Rub the turkey all over with the barbecue seasoning and paprika, then leave to marinate in the fridge overnight.

2. Heat the oil in a frying pan and sear the turkey thighs all over until nicely coloured.

3. Transfer the turkey to a slow cooker and pour in the stock. Cover and cook on low for 6 hours.

4. Shred the turkey into the stock with two forks and sprinkle with chillies.

5. Serve with potato wedges.

Chickpeas with merguez

SERVES: 4 | PREP TIME: 15 MINUTES | COOKING TIME: 4 HOURS 30 MINUTES

INGREDIENTS

200 g / 7 oz / 1 ⅓ cups dried chickpeas,
soaked overnight

2 tbsp olive oil

12 merguez sausages

1 onion, quartered and sliced

2 red peppers, halved and sliced

2 cloves of garlic, sliced

2 tbsp flat leaf parsley, chopped

METHOD

1. Drain the chickpeas of their soaking water,
   then tip them into a saucepan, cover with
   cold water and bring to the boil. Cook for 10
   minutes then drain well.

2. Transfer the chickpeas to a slow cooker and
   add enough cold water to cover
   them by 5 cm (2 inches).

3. Cover and cook on high for 4 hours or until
   the chickpeas are tender.

4. Towards the end of the cooking time, heat
   the oil in a frying pan and colour
   the merguez all over. Transfer to a chopping
   board and cut into short lengths.

5. Add the onions and peppers to the frying
   pan and cook over a low heat for
   15 minutes, stirring occasionally. Add the
   garlic and cook for another 5 minutes.

6. Drain the chickpeas of their cooking liquor,
   reserving 350 ml. Return the chickpeas to
   the slow cooker and add the merguez,
   reserved cooking liquor and the contents of
   the frying pan.

7. Cover and cook on low for 30 minutes, then
   stir in the parsley and serve.

Beef brisket with beetroot

SERVES: 4-6 | PREP TIME: 15 MINUTES | COOKING TIME: 6 HOURS

INGREDIENTS

1 kg / 2 lb 3 oz beef brisket

1 tbsp smoked paprika

1 tbsp dried oregano

1 tbsp garlic granules

1 tbsp cumin

300 g / 10 ½ oz beetroot, peeled and quartered

4 cloves of garlic

2 tsp olive oil

400 g / 14 oz / 2 cups brown rice

100 g / 3 ½ oz / ⅔ cup peas, frozen

handful of flat leaf parsley, chopped

METHOD

1. Preheat the oven to 140°C (120°C fan) / 275F / gas 1.

2. Rub the beef all over with the paprika, oregano, garlic and cumin before seasoning with salt and black pepper. Wrap tightly with a double layer of foil and place onto a baking tray.

3. Place the meat into the oven and roast for 5-6 hours. Remove from the oven and shred the meat into the cooking juices.

4. Mix the beetroot, garlic and oil in a roasting tray and place into the oven once the meat has been cooking for 3 hours. Leave to roast for up to 2 hours until tender. Remove from the oven and roughly chop the beetroot.

5. Mix the beetroot and shredded beef together and season to taste.

6. Cook the rice as per the packet instructions, set aside until needed.

7. Cook the peas in a pan of boiling water for 6-8 minutes until tender. Drain and mix into the rice along with the parsley.

8. Serve the rice with the beef and beetroot.

Smoked ham hock

SERVES: 2-4 | PREP TIME: 4 MINUTES | COOKING TIME: 3 HOURS

INGREDIENTS

2 x smoked ham hocks

ground sea salt

freshly ground black pepper

METHOD

1. Place the ham hocks into a bowl of water. Cover and leave for at least 4 hours or overnight to draw out the salt.

2. Remove from the water and pat dry with kitchen paper.

3. Preheat the oven to 240°C (220°C fan) / 475F / gas 9.

4. Score the skin of the ham hocks and rub with salt and black pepper.

5. Place into the hot oven and roast for 12-15 minutes until the skin is starting to blister.

6. Turn the heat down to 150°C (130°C fan) / 300F / gas 2, cover tightly with foil and roast for 3 hours.

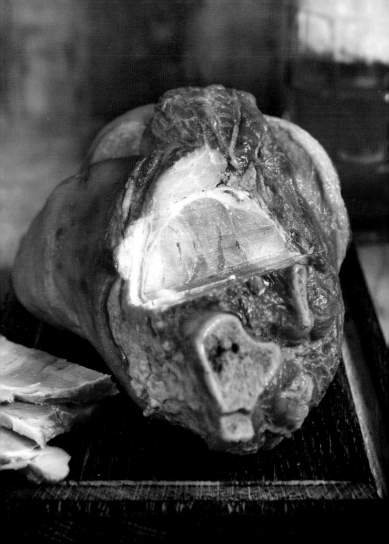

Roast beef sandwich

SERVES: 4-6 | PREP TIME: 15 MINUTES | COOKING TIME: 3 HOURS

INGREDIENTS

800 g / 1 lb 12 oz topside beef

4 shallots, peeled and halved

1 bulb of garlic, halved

300 ml / 10 fl. oz / 1 ¼ cup reduced salt beef stock

1 crusty loaf, sliced

METHOD

1. Preheat the oven to 140°C (120°C fan) / 275F / gas 1.

2. Trim the beef of any excess fat, and place into a roasting tray with the shallots and garlic placed underneath.

3. Season with salt and black pepper before pouring over the beef stock. Cover the beef and roasting tray with foil and place into the oven for up to 3 hours. Remove to rest for 30 minutes before carving.

4. Place the beef onto the sliced bread, spoon over some of the juices from the roasting tray.

Pulled pork roll

SERVES: 4-6 | PREP TIME: 20 MINUTES | COOKING TIME: 6 HOURS

INGREDIENTS

800 g / 1lb 12 oz pork loin joint

1 tbsp smoked paprika

1 tbsp garlic powder

400 g / 14 oz canned chopped tomatoes

50 g / 1 ¾ oz unsweetened apple sauce

2 tbsp fruit syrup

2 tbsp plain (all-purpose) flour

6 ciabatta rolls

2 tomatoes, sliced

1 red onion, sliced

½ lettuce, leaves washed

METHOD

1. Rub the pork all over with the spices and garlic powder.

2. Place the pork into a slow cooker with the tomatoes, apple sauce and fruit syrup and cook on the low setting for 5 - 6 hours.

3. Remove the pork from the slow cooker and pull apart with forks. Whisk the flour into the sauce to thicken and season to taste.

4. Fill the rolls with the pork and salad ingredients, spooning some of the sauce into the roll.

123

One pot chicken and rice

SERVES: 2 | PREP TIME: 10 MINUTES | COOKING TIME: 2 HOURS

INGREDIENTS

2 large chicken thighs

1 tbsp olive oil

1 onion, diced

2 peppers, sliced

2 cloves of garlic, minced

1 tsp chilli (chili) flakes

1 tsp cumin

200 g / 7 oz / 1 cup brown rice

400 ml / 13 ½ fl. oz / 1⅔ cups reduced salt chicken stock

METHOD

1. Preheat the oven to 160°C (140°C fan) / 325F / gas 3.

2. Heat the oil in a pot with a lid over a medium heat. Season the chicken and place skin side down in the pan. Cook for 2-3 minutes until golden, turn over and cook for a further 2-3 minutes before removing and setting aside.

3. Add the onion to the pan and cook for 5-6 minutes until soft and translucent. Add the peppers, garlic, chilli and cumin and cook for a further minute until fragrant.

4. Add the rice to the pan and mix through the onions and peppers.

5. Return the chicken to the pan before pouring in the stock. Cover and cook in the oven for 1 hours and 45 minutes, or until the rice has absorbed the liquid and is tender.

Thai red curry

SERVES: 2-4 | PREP TIME: 10 MINUTES | COOKING TIME: 3 HOURS

INGREDIENTS

1 tbsp coconut oil

2 shallots, diced

2 cloves of garlic, chopped

2 tbsp Thai red curry paste

400 g / 14 oz chicken breast, diced

400 ml / 13 ½ fl. oz / 1 ⅔ cups low fat coconut milk

4 kaffir lime leaves

METHOD

1. Preheat the oven to 160°C (140°C fan) / 325F / gas 3.

2. Heat the oil in an ovenproof casserole and fry the shallots and garlic to 2-3 minutes until fragrant.

3. Add the curry paste and mix through the vegetables. Add the chicken to the pan and fry to colour for a couple of minutes.

4. Pour the coconut into the pan and add the lime leaves. Stir to combine before covering and placing in the oven for up to 3 hours.

5. Remove from the oven and serve with rice or bread.

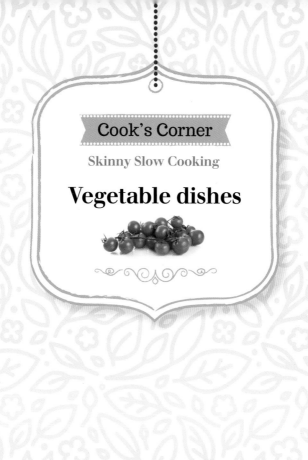

Cook's Corner

Skinny Slow Cooking

Vegetable dishes

Vegetarian cottage pie

SERVES: 2-4 | PREP TIME: 15 MINUTES | COOKING TIME: 1 HOUR

INGREDIENTS

low calorie cooking spray

1 onion, diced

4 carrots, peeled and cubed

2 turnips, peeled and cubed

2 cloves of garlic, minced

500 g / 1 lb 1 oz mushrooms, chopped

400 g / 14 oz canned green lentils, drained

400 g / 14 oz sweet potatoes, peeled and cubed

METHOD

1. Preheat the oven to 160°C (140°C fan) / 325F / gas 3.

2. Place a large casserole pan onto a medium heat and spray with oil. Add the onions and cook for 3-4 minutes until softened. Add the carrots and turnips to the pan and cook for a further 3-4 minutes.

3. Add the garlic to the pan and mix through the other vegetables for a minute before adding the mushrooms. Cook for 2-3 minutes until the mushrooms have softened and started to release some liquid.

4. Add the lentils to the pan and top up with enough liquid to not quite cover the ingredients. Cover and simmer for 12-15 minutes. Season to taste.

5. Cook the sweet potatoes in a pan of boiling water until soft, roughly 20 minutes. Drain and mash until smooth, alternatively place into a blender and blend until smooth. Season with salt and black pepper.

6. Spoon the mushroom and lentil mixture into individual or one large ovenproof dish. Top with the sweet potato mash. Bake in the oven for 1 hour until the top has started to colour.

Tomato and mozzarella tarts

SERVES: 4 | PREP TIME: 30 MINUTES | COOKING TIME: 1 HOUR

INGREDIENTS

150 g / 5 ¼ oz / 1 cup plain (all-purpose) flour

75 g / 2 ½ oz / ⅓ cup butter

1 egg

2 tbsp light green pesto

250 g / 9 oz light mozzarella

2 cloves of garlic, minced

handful of fresh basil, chopped

150 g / 5 ¼ oz cherry tomatoes, halved

METHOD

1. Preheat the oven to 220°C (200°C fan) / 425F / gas 7.

2. Place the flour and butter into a food processor and pulse until the mixture resembles breadcrumbs. Place into a bowl and mix through the egg using a knife until the mixture starts to come together. You may also need to add a splash of cold water.

3. Turn out onto a lightly floured surface and knead to a smooth dough. Roll into a ball and wrap in cling film before placing in the refrigerator to rest for 20 minutes.

4. Remove from the refrigerator and roll out to around 3mm thickness. Cut out into circles to fit into four tartlets cases. Prick the base with a fork and line with a square of greaseproof paper, weighed down with baking beans.

5. Bake in the oven for 15 minutes until golden, remove and set aside to cool. Turn the oven down to 180°C (160°C fan) / 350F / gas 4.

6. Whip together the pesto, mozzarella, garlic and basil. Spoon into the cases and top with the tomatoes.

7. Place into the oven and cook for 25-30 minutes or until the tomatoes have roasted and the tarts have set.

Mushroom quiche

SERVES: 8 | PREP TIME: 45 MINUTES | COOKING TIME: 3 HOURS, 30 MINUTES

INGREDIENTS

110 g / 4 oz / ½ cup reduced fat baking spread, cubed and chilled

225 g / 8 oz / 1 ½ cups plain (all-purpose) flour

2 tbsp olive oil

1 onion, finely chopped

200 g / 7 oz / 2 ⅔ cups button mushrooms, sliced

2 cloves of garlic, sliced

2 tbsp fresh thyme leaves, plus extra to garnish

4 large eggs, beaten

225 ml / 8 fl. oz / ¾ cup skimmed milk

75 g / 2 ½ oz / ½ cup reduced fat cheese, grated

METHOD

1. To make the pastry, rub the baking spread into the flour until the mixture resembles fine breadcrumbs. Stir in just enough cold water to bring the pastry together into a pliable dough, then chill for 30 minutes.

2. Roll out the pastry and use it to line a round flan dish that will fit inside your slow cooker. Cover and cook on high for 2 hours

3. Heat the oil in a large sauté pan and sauté the onion and mushrooms for 10 minutes. Add the garlic and thyme and cook for 2 minutes, then set aside.

4. Whisk the eggs with the milk then stir in the mushroom mixture and cheese. Season generously with salt and pepper.

5. Pour the filling into the pastry case, then cover and cook on low for 1 hour 30 minutes or until the quiche is set in the centre.

6. For a golden finish, colour the top under a hot grill for a few minutes.

Pesto pasta bake

SERVES: 4 | PREP TIME: 15 MINUTES | COOKING TIME: 3 HOURS

INGREDIENTS

2 tbsp reduced fat baking spread

2 tbsp plain (all-purpose) flour

600 ml / 1 pint / 2 ½ cups skimmed milk

150 g / 5 ½ oz / ⅔ cup fresh pesto

400 g / 14 oz / 4 cups dried conchiglie pasta

100 g / 3 ½ oz / 1 cup reduced fat Cheddar, grated

METHOD

1. Put the baking spread, flour and milk in a saucepan. Stir over a medium heat until it bubbles and thickens, then stir in the pesto. Season with salt and pepper to taste.

2. Tip the pasta and sauce into a small slow cooker and stir well. Cover and cook on medium for 3 hours or until the pasta is cooked.

3. Sprinkle over the cheese and cook under a hot grill for a few minutes to brown and crisp the top.

Ratatouille

SERVES: 6 | PREP TIME: 5 MINUTES | COOKING TIME: 3 HOURS

INGREDIENTS

1 aubergine (eggplant), cubed

2 courgettes (zucchini), quartered and sliced

2 red peppers, deseeded and sliced

1 onion, finely chopped

2 cloves of garlic, crushed

1 tbsp fresh thyme leaves

50 ml / 1 ¾ fl. oz / ¼ cup olive oil

6 tomatoes, cut into wedges

250 ml / 9 fl. oz / 1 cup dry white wine

METHOD

1. Mix all of the ingredients, except for the tomatoes and wine, in a slow cooker and season with salt and pepper.

2. Cover the slow cooker and cook on high for 2 hours, stirring every 30 minutes.

3. Add the tomatoes and wine and continue to cook for 1 hour or until the vegetables are tender.

4. Taste again for seasoning and add more salt or pepper if needed.

Vegetable rainbow bake

SERVES: 6 | PREP TIME: 15 MINUTES | COOKING TIME: 3 HOURS

INGREDIENTS

2 Japanese aubergines (eggplants)

3 courgettes (zucchini)

8 tomatoes, same diameter as the aubergines
and courgettes

250 ml / 9 fl. oz / 1 cup dry white wine

2 cloves of garlic, finely chopped

1 tsp cumin seeds

2 tbsp olive oil

parsley, to garnish

METHOD

1. Cut the aubergines, courgettes and tomatoes
   into 5 mm slices.

2. Pack them tightly into a slow cooker,
   alternating between the different
   vegetables as you go.

3. Put the wine, garlic, cumin and oil into a
   glass jar with a pinch of salt and pepper.

4. Screw on the lid and shake, then pour the
   mixture all over the vegetables.

5. Cover the slow cooker and cook on medium
   for 3 hours or until the vegetables are tender.

6. Garnish with parsley and serve immediately.

Kidney bean and potato curry

SERVES: 6 | PREP TIME: 16 MINUTES | COOKING TIME: 7 HOURS

INGREDIENTS

250 g / 9 oz / 1 ⅔ cups dried kidney beans, soaked overnight

1 onion, finely chopped

2 cloves of garlic, crushed

1 tbsp fresh root ginger, grated

1 tbsp curry powder

400 g / 14 oz / 2 cups canned tomatoes, chopped

400 g / 14 oz / 2 cups light coconut milk

2 medium potatoes, diced

2 courgettes (zucchini), halved and sliced

boiled rice, to serve

METHOD

1. Drain the beans from their soaking water and put them in a large saucepan of cold water. Bring to the boil and cook for 10 minutes, then drain well.

2. Mix the beans with rest of the ingredients in a slow cooker, then cover and cook on medium for 7 hours. Add a little boiling water if it starts to look dry at any point.

3. Season to taste with salt and pepper, then serve with boiled rice.

Roasted new potatoes

SERVES: 6 | PREP TIME: 15 MINUTES | COOKING TIME: 4 HOURS

INGREDIENTS

50 ml / 1 ¾ fl. oz / ¼ cup olive oil

3 cloves of garlic, unpeeled

2 sprigs rosemary

900 g / 2 lb small new potatoes,
scrubbed and halved

1 small bunch dill, chopped

METHOD

1. Put the oil in a slow cooker with the garlic
and rosemary and heat on high for
15 minutes.

2. Stir in the potatoes and season with salt and
pepper, then cook on medium for
4 hours, stirring once an hour. They are
ready when a skewer slides in easily and they
are starting to brown on the outside.

3. Sprinkle the potatoes with dill and
serve immediately.

Garlic butter aubergines

SERVES: 4 | PREP TIME: 10 MINUTES | COOKING TIME: 3 HOURS

INGREDIENTS

2 aubergines (eggplants), halved lengthways

2 tbsp butter, softened

2 tbsp olive oil

2 tbsp flat leaf parsley, finely chopped

2 cloves of garlic, crushed

METHOD

1. Score the inside of flesh of the aubergines to make a diamond pattern.

2. Beat the butter with the oil, parsley and garlic and season with salt and pepper.

3. Spread the mixture all over the cut side of the aubergines, then arrange them, cut side up in a single layer in a slow cooker.

4. Cover and cook on medium for 3 hours or until a knife slides into the thickest part of the flesh with little resistance.

Cauliflower cheese

SERVES: 4 | PREP TIME: 15 MINUTES | COOKING TIME: 3 HOURS

INGREDIENTS

2 tbsp reduced fat cooking spread

2 tbsp plain (all-purpose) flour

600 ml / 1 pint / 2 ½ cups skimmed milk

1 tbsp Dijon mustard

1 tsp paprika

150 g / 5 ½ oz / 1 ½ cups reduced fat Cheddar, grated

1 large cauliflower, broken into florets

1 tbsp basil, finely chopped

METHOD

1. Put the cooking spread, flour and milk in a saucepan set over a medium heat.
   Stir until the sauce thickens and starts to bubble. Take the pan off the heat and stir in the mustard, paprika and half the cheese.

2. Arrange the cauliflower in a slow cooker then pour over the sauce.

3. Cook on medium for 3 hours or until the cauliflower is al dente.

4. Sprinkle the rest of the cheese on top and colour it under a hot grill before serving, sprinkled with basil.

Baked artichokes

SERVES: 4 | PREP TIME: 10 MINUTES | COOKING TIME: 3 HOURS

INGREDIENTS

4 globe artichokes, trimmed and chokes removed

1 lemon, juiced

4 cloves of garlic, peeled

50 ml / 1 ¾ fl. oz / ¼ cup olive oil

METHOD

1. Sprinkle the artichokes inside and out with lemon juice and season with salt and pepper.

2. Sit each artichoke on a large square of foil and push a garlic clove into each one. Drizzle with oil, then enclose each artichoke in the foil and scrunch to secure.

3. Arrange the artichokes in a snug single layer in a slow cooker and pour 2.5 cm (1 inch) boiling water into the bottom. Cover and cook on high for 3 hours.

4. Carefully unwrap the artichokes and check that they are tender before serving.

141

Potato gratin

SERVES: 4 | PREP TIME: 20 MINUTES | COOKING TIME: 1 HOUR

INGREDIENTS

750 g / 1 lb 10 oz Maris Piper potatoes

6 cloves of garlic, sliced

600 ml / 20 ¼ fl. oz / 2 ½ cups low fat double (heavy) cream

METHOD

1. Preheat the oven to 180°C (160°C fan) / 350F / gas 4.

2. Peel the potatoes and then thinly slice with a sharp knife or mandoline.

3. Layer the potatoes and garlic in an ovenproof dish, seasoning between each layer.

4. Pour the cream over the top before placing into the oven.

5. Leave to cook in the oven for at least 1 hour, or until the top has browned and the potatoes are tender.

6. Remove and serve hot as a side dish to slow roast meats.

Braised red lentils

SERVES: 6 | PREP TIME: 10 MINUTES | COOKING TIME: 3 HOURS

INGREDIENTS

2 tbsp olive oil

1 onion, finely chopped

2 cloves of garlic, crushed

1 tsp smoked paprika

½ tsp ground cumin

1 tbsp tomato puree

1.2 litres / 2 pint / 5 cups vegetable stock

400 g / 14 oz / 3 ¼ cups red lentils

1 small bunch coriander (cilantro), chopped

METHOD

1. Heat the oil in a frying pan and fry the onion gently for 6 minutes.

2. Add the garlic and cook for 2 minutes, then stir in the spices and tomato puree. Stir over a low heat for 2 minutes, then deglaze with a splash of the vegetable stock.

3. Transfer to a slow cooker and stir in the lentils and ½ teaspoon of salt.

4. Cover and cook on high for 3 hours or until the lentils are tender, but still holding their shape.

5. Taste and adjust the seasoning with salt and pepper, then stir in the coriander and serve.

Borscht

SERVES: 4 | PREP TIME: 15 MINUTES | COOKING TIME: 3 HOURS

INGREDIENTS

1.2 litres / 2 pints / 4 ¾ cups vegetable stock

450 g / 1 lb / 3 ⅔ cups beetroot, peeled and diced

1 bay leaf

2 tsp ground cumin

150 ml / 5 ½ fl. oz / ⅔ cup half fat soured cream

1 handful rocket (arugula)

breadsticks, to serve

METHOD

1. Put the stock, beetroot, bay leaf and cumin in a slow cooker.

2. Cover and cook on high for 3 hours. Discard the bay leaf then ladle the soup into a liquidizer and blend until smooth with the soured cream. Season to taste with salt and pepper.

3. Serve the soup hot or chilled, with a few rocket leaves on top and some breadsticks on the side.

Roast peppers

SERVES: 2-4 | PREP TIME: 15 MINUTES | COOKING TIME: 1 HOUR

INGREDIENTS

3 red peppers

3 yellow peppers

10 cloves of garlic, bruised

4 shallots, roughly chopped

METHOD

1. Preheat the oven to 160°C (140°C fan) / 325F / gas 3.

2. Roughly slice the peppers and remove the seeds and membrane.

3. Toss the peppers with the garlic and shallots.

4. Place into a baking tray and roast, uncovered, for 1 hour until tender and aromatic.

Porcini risotto

SERVES: 4 | PREP TIME: 20 MINUTES | COOKING TIME: 2 HOURS

INGREDIENTS

2 tbsp olive oil

225 g / 8 oz / 3 cups small porcini mushrooms, or a
mixture of porcini and chestnut mushrooms

300 g / 10 ½ oz / 1 ½ cups risotto rice

150 ml / 5 ½ fl. oz / ⅔ cup dry white wine

3 shallots, finely chopped

3 cloves of garlic, finely chopped

2 tbsp dried porcini mushrooms, soaked in boiling
water for 20 minutes

750 ml / 1 pints 5 ½ fl. oz / 3 cups vegetable stock

50 g / 1 ¾ oz / ½ cup Parmesan, finely grated

2 tbsp flat leaf parsley, chopped

2 tbsp Parmesan shavings

METHOD

1. Heat the oil in a sauté pan and fry the
mushrooms for 8 minutes. Reserve a few
whole mushrooms for the garnish and slice
the rest. Set aside.

2. Stir the rice into the sauté pan and toast
gently for 2 minutes. Add the wine and boil
vigorously until almost completely
evaporated, then scrape the mixture into a
slow cooker. Add the shallots, garlic, dried
porcini and vegetable stock. Cover and cook
on high for 2 hours or until the rice is tender.

3. Stir in the sliced mushrooms, grated
Parmesan and parsley and leave to stand for
5 minutes. Stir well and serve, garnished
with the mushrooms and Parmesan.

Baked eggs with peppers

SERVES: 4 | PREP TIME: 5 MINUTES | COOKING TIME: 4 HOURS

INGREDIENTS

2 tbsp olive oil

1 red onion, sliced

2 red peppers, sliced

2 yellow peppers, sliced

2 cloves of garlic, sliced

250 g / 9 oz / 1 ⅔ cups small
tomatoes, quartered

1 tsp dried oregano

250 ml / 9 fl. oz / 1 cup vegetable stock

4 large eggs

a few sprigs fresh oregano

METHOD

1. Put the oil in a slow cooker and heat on high.
   Stir in the onion and peppers and season
   with salt and pepper. Cover and cook for 1
   hour 30 minutes, stirring every 15 minutes.

2. Stir in the garlic, tomatoes, dried oregano
   and stock.

3. Cover and cook on low for 2 hours. Season
   with salt and pepper and stir well,
   then break in the eggs.

4. Cover and cook for 30 minutes or until the
   egg whites have set.

5. Carefully spoon the eggs and peppers into
   four bowls and garnish with fresh oregano.

Lentil and root vegetable bake

SERVES: 2-4 | PREP TIME: 30 MINUTES | COOKING TIME: 45 MINUTES

INGREDIENTS

low calorie cooking spray

2 onions, sliced

2 cloves of garlic, minced

4 carrots, peeled and cubed

4 potatoes, peeled and cubed

2 turnips, peeled and cubed

2 tbsp thyme leaves

400 g / 14 oz canned green lentils, drained

500 ml / 17 fl. oz / 2 cups low salt vegetable stock

100 g / 3 ½ oz / ⅔ cup panko breadcrumbs

METHOD

1. Preheat the oven to 160°C (140°C fan) / 325F / gas 3.

2. Place a large casserole pan onto a medium heat and spray with oil. Add the onions and cook for 3-4 minutes until softened. Add the garlic and cook for a further minute.

3. Add the carrots, potatoes, turnips and thyme to the pan and cook for a further 3-4 minutes.

4. Add the lentils to the pan and pour in the stock. Cover and simmer for 12-15 minutes. Season to taste. Pour into an ovenproof dish and top with the breadcrumbs.

5. Bake in the oven for 45 minutes.

Wild rice and courgette pilaf

SERVES: 4 | PREP TIME: 10 MINUTES | COOKING TIME: 4 HOURS

INGREDIENTS

2 tbsp olive oil

6 spring onions (scallions), chopped, green and white parts separated

2 cloves of garlic, finely chopped

450 g / 1 lb / 2 ¼ cups mixed brown and wild rice

750 ml / 1 pint 5 ½ fl. oz / 3 cups vegetable stock

1 tsp ground cumin

1 tsp ground coriander

2 courgettes (zucchini), sliced

125 g / 4 ½ oz / 1 ball light mozzarella, grated

METHOD

1. Heat the oil in a frying pan and stir-fry the spring onion whites and garlic for 5 minutes. Add the rice and stir for 2 minutes to toast, then scrape it into a slow cooker.

2. Stir in the stock, spices and courgette, then cover and cook on high for 4 hours or until the rice is tender.

3. Season to taste with salt and pepper, then spoon into four heatproof bowls. Sprinkle over the mozzarella and toast under a hot grill for a few minutes to melt.

4. Garnish with spring onion greens and serve immediately.

149

Sweet pumpkin rice

SERVES: 1 | PREP TIME: 30 MINUTES | COOKING TIME: 2 HOUR

INGREDIENTS

50 g / 1 ¾ oz / ¼ cup brown rice

150 g / 5 ¼ oz pumpkin

100 ml / 3 ½ fl. oz / ½ cup almond milk

50 g / 1 ¾ oz / ⅓ cup redcurrants

METHOD

1. Soak the rice in cold water for 30 minutes.

2. Drain the rice and then cook as per the packet instructions. Drain and set aside.

3. Peel the pumpkin and roughly chop the flesh.

4. Cook the pumpkin slow cooker with the milk on the high setting for 2 hours until tender.

5. Blend together the rice, pumpkin and milk. Place into a saucepan and gently heat to warm through. Pour into a serving bowl and top with the redcurrants.

Melanzane alla parmigiana

SERVES: 4 | PREP TIME: 15 MINUTES | COOKING TIME: 4 HOURS

INGREDIENTS

400 g / 14 oz / 2 cups canned tomatoes, chopped

1 small onion, finely chopped

2 cloves of garlic, finely chopped

1 tbsp parsley, chopped, plus extra to garnish

2 aubergines, sliced lengthways

250 g / 9 oz / 2 balls light mozzarella, grated

25 g Parmesan, finely grated

METHOD

1. Mix the canned tomatoes with the onion, garlic and parsley and season with salt and pepper.

2. Layer up the tomato mixture with the aubergines and grated mozzarella in a small slow cooker.

3. Sprinkle the top with Parmesan, then cover and cook on medium for 4 hours.

4. If you prefer, the top can be coloured under a hot grill just before serving.

Filo pies with veggie filling

SERVES: 4 | PREP TIME: 30 MINUTES | COOKING TIME: 3 HOURS, 30 MINUTES

INGREDIENTS

½ small butternut squash, peeled deseeded and diced

1 courgette (zucchini), diced

½ tbsp fresh root ginger, grated

2 cloves of garlic, crushed

1 tsp ground cumin

1 tsp ground cinnamon

250 ml / 9 fl. oz / 1 cup vegetable stock

2 tbsp pine nuts, toasted

75 g / 2 ½ oz / ½ cup feta cheese, diced

12 squares filo pastry

50 g / 1 ¾ oz / ¼ cup reduced fat cooking spread, melted

METHOD

1. Toss the squash and courgette with the ginger, garlic, cumin and cinnamon in a small slow cooker. Pour over the stock and cook on high for 3 hours or until the vegetables are tender and the liquid has been absorbed.

2. Leave the filling to cool, then stir in the pine nuts and feta.

3. Preheat the oven to 200°C (180°C fan) / 400F / gas 6.

4. Brush the filo squares with cooking spread and layer them up in threes. Use each set to line a hole of a large muffin tin.

5. Spoon in the filling to come level with the top of the tin, then bring the pastry sides up and scrunch to seal.

6. Bake the pies for 20 minutes or until the pastry is crisp and golden brown.

Rice stuffed squash

SERVES: 2 | PREP TIME: 30 MINUTES | COOKING TIME: 4 HOURS

INGREDIENTS

1 medium butternut squash, halved and deseeded

1 litre / 1 pint 15 fl. oz / 4 cups vegetable stock

2 tbsp olive oil

2 shallots, finely chopped

3 cloves of garlic, crushed

150 g / 5 ½ oz / ¾ cup risotto rice

50 g / 1 ¾ oz / ½ cup Parmesan, finely grated

small bunch parsley, finely chopped

METHOD

1. Use a melon baller to gouge some of the squash flesh from the neck end, so that the cavity runs the whole length of the squash. Reserve the scooped out flesh and put the two squash halves into a snugly fitting slow cooker.

2. Heat the stock in a saucepan and keep it just below simmering point.

3. Heat the olive oil in a sauté pan and gently fry the shallots and garlic for 8 minutes or until golden, then stir in the rice and reserved squash flesh.

4. When it is well coated with the oil, add half of the stock and cook for 8 minutes, stirring occasionally. Stir in the rest of the stock and cook for 5 minutes, then stir in the Parmesan and parsley.

5. Fill the squash shells with the par-cooked risotto, then pour enough boiling water into the slow cooker to come half way up the sides of the squash.

6. Cover and cook on high for 4 hours or until a skewer slides easily into the squash

Quinoa salad

SERVES: 4 | PREP TIME: 15 MINUTES | COOKING TIME: 4 HOURS

INGREDIENTS

200 g / 7 oz quinoa

400 ml / 13 ½ fl. oz / 1 ⅔ cups reduced salt chicken stock

150 g / 5 ¼ oz cherry tomatoes, halved

75 g / 2 ½ oz / ½ cup black olives, pitted

1 lemon, juiced

100 g / 3 ½ oz low fat feta, diced

small bunch of flat leaf parsley, chopped

METHOD

1. Rinse the quinoa with cold water.

2. Place the quinoa and stock into a slow cooker and set to high.

3. After 4 hours the quinoa should be cooked and tender.

4. Combine the quinoa with the remaining ingredients and serve.

Pear and stilton quiches

SERVES: 4 | PREP TIME: 15 MINUTES | COOKING TIME: 3 HOURS

INGREDIENTS

250 g / 9 oz puff pastry

3 large eggs

200 ml / 7 fl. oz / ¾ cup skimmed milk

100 g / 3 ½ oz / 1 cup stilton, diced

1 pear, cut into 4 thick slices

METHOD

1. Roll out the pastry and use it to line four mini casserole dishes which will fit inside your slow cooker in an even layer.

2. Gently whisk the eggs with the milk until smoothly combined then stir in the stilton and season with black pepper. Pour the mixture into the pastry cases and stand a pear slice up in each one.

3. Transfer the dishes to the slow cooker. Cover the slow cooker with a clean tea towel, then put on the lid and cook on high for 3 hours.

4. The quiches can be finished in a hot oven to crisp the pastry and brown the tops.

Cauliflower curry

SERVES: 6 | PREP TIME: 15 MINUTES | COOKING TIME: 3 HOURS, 30 MINUTES

INGREDIENTS

2 tbsp sunflower oil

1 onion, finely chopped

2 cloves of garlic, crushed

1 tbsp fresh root ginger, grated

1 tbsp curry powder

2 tbsp tomato puree

400 g / 14 oz / 2 cups canned tomatoes, chopped

400 g / 14 oz / 2 cups light coconut milk

1 cauliflower, broken into large florets

50 g / 1 ¾ oz / ½ cup ground almonds

150 g / 5 ½ oz / 1 cup peas

METHOD

1. Heat the oil in a frying pan and fry the onion, garlic and ginger over a low heat for 8 minutes. Add the curry powder and tomato puree and stir for 2 minutes.

2. Stir in 100 ml of water, then scrape everything into a slow cooker. Add the canned tomatoes and coconut milk, then stir in the cauliflower.

3. Cover and cook on medium for 3 hours. Stir in the ground almonds and peas, then cover and cook for another 30 minutes. Season to taste.

Squash and chickpea stew

SERVES: 4 | PREP TIME: 15 MINUTES | COOKING TIME: 4 HOURS

INGREDIENTS

200 g / 7 oz / 1 ⅓ cups dried chickpeas, soaked overnight

2 acorn squashes, peeled, deseeded and diced (or 1 small butternut squash)

400 g / 14 oz / 2 cups canned tomatoes, chopped

50 g / 1 ¾ oz / ¼ cup mixed brown and wild rice

500 ml / 17 ½ fl. oz / 2 cups vegetable stock

1 onion, finely chopped

1 celery stick, finely chopped

2 carrots, diced

2 cloves of garlic, finely chopped

1 tsp ground cumin

1 tsp smoked paprika

METHOD

1. Drain the chickpeas of their soaking water, then tip them into a saucepan, cover with cold water and bring to the boil. Cook for 10 minutes then drain well.

2. Transfer the chickpeas to a slow cooker and stir in the rest of the ingredients, except for the chives.

3. Cover and cook on high for 4 hours or until the chickpeas and squash are tender.

4. Season to taste with salt and pepper, then ladle into four warm bowls and serve garnished with chives.

Red pepper risotto

SERVES: 4 | PREP TIME: 30 MINUTES | COOKING TIME: 1 HOUR

INGREDIENTS

2 tbsp olive oil

1 onion, finely chopped

2 red peppers, finely chopped

2 cloves of garlic, finely chopped

1 tsp smoked paprika

300 g / 10 ½ oz / 1 ½ cups risotto rice

2 medium tomatoes, finely chopped

150 ml / 5 ½ fl. oz / ⅔ cup dry white wine

750 ml / 1 pints 5 ½ fl. oz / 3 cups vegetable stock

50 g / 1 ¾ oz / 1 ½ cups rocket (arugula)

50 g / 1 ¾ oz / ½ cup Parmesan, finely grated

1 lemon, cut into wedges

METHOD

1. Heat the oil in a frying pan and fry the onion and peppers over a low heat for 18 minutes. Add the garlic and paprika and stir-fry for 2 minutes.

2. Add the rice and stir over a low heat for 3 minutes to toast it, then pour in the wine and add the tomato and bubble for 2 minutes.

3. Scrape the contents of the pan into a slow cooker, add the stock and stir well. Cover and cook on high for 2 hours or until the rice is cooked. Stir well and season, then spoon into four warm bowls and garnish with rocket, Parmesan and lemon wedges.

Vegetable pasta bake

SERVES: 4 | PREP TIME: 15 MINUTES | COOKING TIME: 3 HOURS

INGREDIENTS

2 tbsp reduced fat baking spread

2 tbsp plain (all-purpose) flour

600 ml / 1 pint / 2 ½ cups skimmed milk

1 tbsp Dijon mustard

100 g / 3 ½ oz / 1 cup reduced fat Cheddar, grated

½ cauliflower, broken into florets

½ broccoli, broken into florets

300 g / 10 ½ oz / 3 cups fusilli

125 g / 4 ½ oz / 1 ball light mozzarella, diced

½ tsp dried oregano

1 handful basil leaves

METHOD

1. Put the baking spread, flour and milk in a saucepan. Stir over a medium heat until it bubbles and thickens, then stir in the mustard and cheddar. Season with salt and pepper to taste.

2. Toss the cauliflower, broccoli and fusilli with the sauce in a slow cooker and top with mozzarella and oregano. Cover and cook on medium for 3 hours or until the vegetables are al dente and the pasta is cooked.

3. Garnish with basil leaves and serve immediately.

161

Squash risotto

SERVES: 4 | PREP TIME: 20 MINUTES | COOKING TIME: 2 HOURS

INGREDIENTS

1 small crown prince squash, peeled,
deseeded and diced

300 g / 10 ½ oz / 1 ½ cups risotto rice

150 ml / 5 ½ fl. oz / ⅔ cup dry white wine

2 shallots, finely chopped

2 cloves of garlic, finely chopped

750 ml / 1 pints 5 ½ fl. oz / 3 cups vegetable stock

¼ tsp nutmeg, freshly ground

50 g / 1 ¾ oz / ½ cup Parmesan, finely grated

METHOD

1. Mix all of the ingredients together in a slow
   cooker, except for the Parmesan.
   Cover and cook on high for 2 hours or until
   the rice and squash are both tender.

2. Stir in the Parmesan and leave to stand,
   uncovered for 5 minutes.

3. Stir well then spoon into four warm bowls
   and serve immediately.

Cauliflower and paneer curry

SERVES: 2-4 | PREP TIME: 15 MINUTES | COOKING TIME: 1 HOUR

INGREDIENTS

1 tsp olive oil

1 onion, diced

1 clove of garlic, minced

2 chillies (chili), chopped

1 head of cauliflower, florets

200 g / 7 oz paneer

2 tsp curry powder

1 tsp fenugreek

500 ml / 17 fl. oz / 2 cups low salt chicken stock

METHOD

1. Heat the oil in a large casserole with a lid over a moderate heat. Add the onion and cook for 4-5 minutes until softened. Add the garlic and chillies to the pan and cook for a further minute until fragrant.

2. Add the cauliflower, paneer, curry powder and fenugreek and mix through the onions, chilli and garlic. Cook for 4-5 minutes.

3. Pour the stock in and heat until boiling. Cover and simmer for 45 minutes.

4. Remove the lid from the pan and increase the heat a little to reduce the sauce. Once thickened, serve.

Stuffing

SERVES: 8 | PREP TIME: 15 MINUTES | COOKING TIME: 4 HOURS

INGREDIENTS

50 ml / 1 ¾ fl. oz / ¼ cup olive oil

2 onions, finely chopped

1 stick celery, finely chopped

2 cloves of garlic, finely chopped

1 handful sage leaves, chopped

1 tbsp rosemary, finely chopped,
plus extra to garnish

300 g / 10 ½ oz / 4 cups fresh white breadcrumbs

6 slices two day old sourdough, crusts removed
and cubed

2 large eggs, beaten

350 ml / 12 fl. oz / 1 ½ cups vegetable stock

low calorie cooking spray

METHOD

1. Heat the oil in a sauté pan and fry the onion
   and celery over a medium heat for 10
   minutes. Add the garlic, sage and rosemary
   and cook for 2 minutes. Take the pan off the
   heat and stir in the breadcrumbs and
   sourdough cubes.

2. Whisk the egg into the stock, then stir it into
   the stuffing and season with salt and pepper.

3. Spray the slow cooker with low calorie
   cooking spray, then scrape in the stuffing.
   Cover and cook on low for 4 hours.

4. Spoon the stuffing into a serving dish and
   garnish with rosemary.

Rice and broccoli bakes

SERVES: 4 | PREP TIME: 15 MINUTES | COOKING TIME: 1 HOUR

INGREDIENTS

2 tbsp olive oil

400 g / 14 oz / 2 cups brown rice

1 onion, diced

2 cloves of garlic, chopped

2 heads of broccoli, florets only

200 g / 7 oz sweetcorn

50 g / 1 ¾ oz / ⅓ cup flour

50 g / 1 ¾ oz / ¼ cup butter

300 ml / 10 fl. oz / 1 ¼ cup skimmed milk

150 g / 5 ¼ oz / 1 ½ cups low fat cheese, grated

200 g / 7 oz / 1 ⅓ cups panko breadcrumbs

METHOD

1. Preheat the oven to 180°C (160°C fan) / 350F / gas 4.

2. Heat half the oil in a pan and add the rice. Cook for 1-2 minutes before adding 800 ml boiling water. Turn the heat down, cover and leave to cook for 30 minutes.

3. Heat the remaining oil in a frying pan. Cook the onions for 4-5 minutes. Add the garlic, broccoli and sweetcorn and cook for a further 2-3 minutes.

4. Heat the butter in a saucepan until melted. Gradually stir in the flour and cook for 2-3 minutes. Add the milk and cheese to make a sauce. Mix the sauce into the rice and vegetables and season. Top with the breadcrumbs and bake for 30 minutes.

Bean and cashew stew

SERVES: 5 | PREP TIME: 20 MINUTES | COOKING TIME: 6 HOURS, 30 MINUTES

INGREDIENTS

250 g / 9 oz / 1 ⅔ cups dried kidney beans,
soaked overnight

250 g / 9 oz / 1 ⅔ cups cashew nuts,
150 g soaked overnight

1 onion, finely chopped

2 cloves of garlic, crushed

1 tbsp fresh root ginger, grated

400 g / 14 oz / 2 cups canned tomatoes, chopped

1 tsp ground coriander seeds

1 tsp cayenne pepper

100 g / 3 ½ oz / 3 cups baby leaf spinach

1 small bunch coriander (cilantro), chopped

METHOD

1. Drain the beans and put them in a large
saucepan of cold water. Bring to the boil and
cook for 10 minutes, then drain well.
Meanwhile, put the 150 g of soaked cashew
nuts in a food processor with 100 ml of water
and blend until smooth.

2. Mix the beans with the cashew puree, onion,
garlic, ginger, tomatoes, coriander and
cayenne pepper, then cover and cook on
medium for 6 hours. Add a little boiling
water if it starts to look dry at any point.

3. Stir in the spinach, coriander and two thirds
of the rest of the cashews and cook for 30
minutes. Season and add the remaining
cashews to serve.

Potato and spinach gratin

SERVES: 4 | PREP TIME: 20 MINUTES | COOKING TIME: 1 HOUR

INGREDIENTS

750 g / 1 lb 10 oz Maris Piper potatoes

200 g / 7 oz spinach, washed

½ tsp nutmeg

handful of flat leaf parsley, chopped

6 cloves of garlic, sliced

600 ml / 20 ¼ fl. oz / 2 ½ cups low fat double (heavy) cream

METHOD

1. Preheat the oven to 180°C (160°C fan) / 350F / gas 4.

2. Peel the potatoes and then thinly slice with a sharp knife or mandoline into discs. Wilt the spinach in a frying pan with the nutmeg. Squeeze out as much of the water from the spinach as possible. Mix the parsley through.

3. Layer the potatoes, spinach and garlic in an ovenproof dish, seasoning between each layer. Pour the cream over the top before placing into the oven.

4. Leave to cook in the oven for at least 1 hour, or until the top has browned and the potatoes are tender.

Roast vegetables with hummus

SERVES: 2-4 | PREP TIME: 15 MINUTES | COOKING TIME: 1 HOUR

INGREDIENTS

4 sweet potatoes, quartered

1 red pepper, sliced

1 head of broccoli, chopped

6 cloves of garlic

1 tbsp coconut oil

400 g / 14 oz canned chickpeas (garbanzo beans)

1 tbsp tahini

1 tbsp low fat mayonnaise

1 tsp ground coriander (cilantro)

1 tsp ground cumin

1 lemon, juice and zest

100 g / 3 ½ oz salad leaves

METHOD

1. Preheat the oven to 160°C (140°C fan) / 325F / gas 3.

2. Place the sweet potatoes, pepper and broccoli into an ovenproof dish with 4 of the cloves of garlic. Add the coconut oil and toss to coat.

3. Place the vegetables into the oven and roast for 1 hour, cover with foil after the first 30 minutes to prevent burning.

4. Drain the chickpeas and place into the cup of a blender with the tahini, mayonnaise, coriander, cumin and lemon. Blend for 1-2 minutes until smooth, season to taste.

5. Serve the hummus with the roasted vegetables and salad.

Vegetable rice

SERVES: 4-6 | PREP TIME: 15 MINUTES | COOKING TIME: 2 HOURS

● ●

INGREDIENTS

250 g / 9 oz / 1 ¼ cups basmati rice

4 carrots, diced

1 head of cauliflower, florets only

1 onion, diced

500 ml / 17 fl. oz / 2 cups low salt vegetable stock

200 g / 7 oz / 1 ⅓ cups garden peas

2 eggs, beaten, fried and cut into squares

METHOD

1. Preheat your slow cooker to the high setting.

2. Place the ingredients, apart from the peas, into the slow cooker and replace the lid.

3. Leave to cook for 1 hour, 40 minutes. Check once or twice towards the end of cooking to ensure the rice is cooked and the liquid has been absorbed.

4. Stir the peas into the rice and replace the lid. Leave for a further 20 minutes, with the heat set to warm.

5. Season and serve either as a side dish or a vegetarian main dish, with the egg.

169

Spinach and feta quiche

SERVES: 8 | PREP TIME: 45 MINUTES | COOKING TIME: 3 HOURS

INGREDIENTS

110 g / 4 oz / ½ cup reduced fat baking spread, cubed and chilled

225 g / 8 oz / 1 ½ cups plain (all-purpose) flour

2 tbsp olive oil

1 onion, finely chopped

2 cloves of garlic, finely chopped

150 g / 5 ½ oz / 4 ½ cups spinach, washed

4 large eggs, beaten

225 ml / 8 fl. oz / ¾ cup skimmed milk

150 g / 5 ½ oz / 1 cup feta, diced

METHOD

1. Rub the baking spread into the flour until the mixture resembles fine breadcrumbs. Stir in just enough cold water to bring the pastry together into a pliable dough, then chill for 30 minutes.

2. Roll out the pastry and use it to line a round cake tin that will fit inside your slow cooker. Cover and cook on high for 1 hour 30 minutes.

3. Heat the oil in a large sauté pan and fry the onion for 8 minutes. Add the garlic and cook for 2 minutes. Pack as much spinach into the pan as you can and put on the lid.

4. Cook for 2 minutes, then stir well and add more spinach. Continue until all the spinach is well wilted, then tip it into a sieve and squeeze out as much liquid as possible.

5. Whisk the eggs with the milk then stir in the spinach mixture and feta. Season with salt and pepper.

6. Pour the filling into the pastry case, then cover and cook on low for 1 hour 30 minutes or until the quiche is set in the centre.

171

Broccoli quiche

SERVES: 8 | PREP TIME: 45 MINUTES | COOKING TIME: 3 HOURS

INGREDIENTS

110 g / 4 oz / ½ cup reduced fat baking spread, cubed and chilled

225 g / 8 oz / 1 ½ cups plain (all-purpose) flour

2 tbsp olive oil

1 large leek, sliced

1 small head broccoli, broken into florets

2 cloves of garlic, sliced

100 g / 3 ½ oz / ½ cup roasted red peppers, drained and chopped

4 large eggs, beaten

225 ml / 8 fl. oz / ¾ cup skimmed milk

75 g / 2 ½ oz / ½ cup reduced fat cheese, grated

METHOD

1. To make the pastry, rub the baking spread into the flour until the mixture resembles fine breadcrumbs. Stir in just enough cold water to bring the pastry together into a pliable dough, then chill for 30 minutes.

2. Roll out the pastry and use it to line the base and 6 cm (2 ½ in) up the sides of a small round slow cooker. Cover and cook on high for 1 hour 30 minutes.

3. Heat the oil in a large sauté pan and sauté the leeks and broccoli for 10 minutes. Add the garlic and cook for 2 minutes, then set aside.

4. Whisk the eggs with the milk then stir in the broccoli mixture. Season generously with salt and pepper.

5. Pour the filling into the pastry case and scatter the cheese on top.

6. Cover and cook on low for 1 hour 30 minutes or until the quiche is set in the centre.

Cook's Corner

Skinny Slow Cooking
Desserts

Berry cheesecake

SERVES: 8 | PREP TIME: 30 MINUTES | COOKING TIME: 3 HOURS

INGREDIENTS

200 g / 7 oz / 2 cups light digestive biscuits, crushed

50 g / 1 ¾ oz / ¼ cup reduced fat baking spread, melted

2 tbsp cacao powder

600 g / 1 lb 5 oz / 2 ¾ cups low fat cream cheese

150 ml / 5 fl. oz / ⅔ cup half fat soured cream

2 large eggs, plus 1 egg yolk

2 tbsp plain (all-purpose) flour

50 g / 1 ¾ oz / ¼ cup stevia

300 g / 10 ½ oz / 2 cups mixed berries

mint leaves, to garnish

METHOD

1. Mix the biscuit crumbs with the baking spread and cacao and press into an even layer in the bottom of a spring-form cake tin that will fit inside your slow cooker.

2. Whisk together the rest of the ingredients, except for the berries, until smooth. Fold in half of the berries, then pour the mixture into the tin and level the surface.

3. Put a rack into the bottom of your slow cooker and add 2.5 cm (1 in) of boiling water, then position the cake tin on top. Cover the top of the slow cooker with 3 layers of kitchen paper before putting on the lid.

4. Cook on high for 2 hours, then turn off the slow cooker and leave to cook in the residual heat without lifting the lid for 1 hour.

5. Take the cheesecake out of the slow cooker and leave to cool to room temperature before chilling for at least 2 hours.

6. Carefully unspring the tin and decorate the top of the cheesecake with berries and mint leaves.

Mini tarte tatin

SERVES: 4 | PREP TIME: 20 MINUTES | COOKING TIME: 1 HOUR

INGREDIENTS

200 g / 7 oz puff pastry

4 dessert apples

100 g / 3 ½ oz date syrup

50 g / 1 ¾ oz low fat butter spread

METHOD

1. Roll out the pastry to roughly 3mm thickness and cut out 4 discs roughly 10 cm / 4 inches in diameter using a tartlet case for reference. Prick with a fork and wrap in cling film before freezing.

2. Preheat the oven to 180°C (160°C fan) / 350F / gas 4.

3. Peel and core the apples before cutting into quarters, place into a pan of water until needed to stop them browning.

4. Place the syrup and spread into a saucepan and heat gently until the butter has melted and the two ingredients can be mixed together to make a caramel.

5. Place the apples into individual tart cases and pour over the caramel.

6. Bake in the oven for 30 minutes before removing and placing the frozen disc of pastry on top of each tart. Tuck the edges around the tart as the pasty defrosts and prick with a fork to let steam escape.

7. Return to the oven and bake for a further 30 minutes until the pasty is crisp and golden.

8. Remove from the oven and allow to cool before turning out.

Apple sponge

SERVES: 6 | PREP TIME: 20 MINUTES | COOKING TIME: 2 HOURS

INGREDIENTS

200 g / 7 oz / ¾ cup caster (superfine) sugar

1 large egg

3 tbsp sunflower oil

1 tsp vanilla extract

150 g / 5 ½ oz / 1 cup plain (all-purpose) flour

½ tsp bicarbonate of (baking) soda

½ tsp baking powder

½ tsp cinnamon

4 apples, peeled, cored and halved

METHOD

1. Whisk the sugar, egg, oil and vanilla extract together with an electric whisk for 4 minutes or until thick. Stir the flour, raising agents and cinnamon together, then fold in the egg mixture.

2. Butter the inside of a small slow cooker and scrape in the cake mixture. Slice the apple halves without cutting all the way through, then press them into the top of the cake mix.

3. Cover the slow cooker with a clean tea towel, then put the lid on and bake on medium for 2 hours.

4. Test the cake by inserting a skewer into the centre – if it comes out clean, the cake is done. Otherwise, continue to cook and check again every 15 minutes until it is ready.

5. Leave to cool completely before cutting and serving.

Skinny chocolate lava cakes

SERVES: 4 | PREP TIME: 20 MINUTES | COOKING TIME: 1 HOUR

INGREDIENTS

low calorie cooking spray

2 tbsp cacao powder

100 g / 3 ½ oz / ⅔ cup dark chocolate, min. 70 % cocoa solids, chopped

100 g / 3 ½ oz / ½ cup reduced fat cooking spread

25 g stevia

2 large eggs, plus 2 egg yolks

1 tbsp plain (all-purpose) flour

METHOD

1. Put a rack inside a slow cooker and add 2.5 cm (1 in) of boiling water, then set it to high.

2. Coat the inside of four ramekins with cooking spray and dust with cacao.

3. Melt the chocolate, cooking spread and stevia together in a saucepan, stirring to dissolve the stevia. Leave to cool a little then beat in the eggs and egg yolks and fold in the flour.

4. Divide the mixture between the ramekins, then transfer them to the slow cooker. Lay 3 layers of kitchen paper over the top of the slow cooker before putting on the lid to absorb the condensed steam.

5. Cook for 1 hour on medium or until the lava cakes are set round the outside, but still molten within.

6. Serve immediately.

Apple strudel

SERVES: 2-4 | PREP TIME: 30 MINUTES | COOKING TIME: 1 HOUR

INGREDIENTS

750 g 1 lb 10 oz dessert apples, peeled and sliced

2 tsp cinnamon

½ lemon, juice and zest

100 g / 3 ½ oz / ½ cup xylitol

75 g / 2 ½ oz / ⅓ cup raisins

50 g / 1 ¾ oz / ½ cup walnuts, chopped

low calorie butter spray

6 filo pastry sheets

1 tbsp icing (confectioners') sugar (optional)

METHOD

1. Preheat the oven to 180°C (160°C fan) / 350F / gas 4 and line a baking tray with greaseproof paper.

2. Combine the apples, cinnamon, lemon, xylitol, raisins and walnuts in a bowl.

3. Place one of the pastry sheets onto a clean dry tea towel. Lightly grease by spraying with the butter spray before placing another sheet on top, repeat until all the sheets have been used.

4. Place the filling along one side of the pastry, leaving a 1 in gap from the edge. Using the tea towel to help, roll into a sausage shape folding the end underneath the strudel.

5. Carefully transfer to the baking tray and spray with some more of the butter stray. Bake in the oven for up to 1 hour until crisp and golden.

6. Remove and allow to cool before dusting with icing sugar.

Strawberry, apple and walnut crumble

SERVES: 6 | PREP TIME: 15 MINUTES | COOKING TIME: 2 HOURS

INGREDIENTS

300 g / 10 ½ oz / 2 cups strawberries, quartered

1 large bramley apple, peeled, cored and chopped

1 tbsp plain (all-purpose) flour

1 tsp ground cinnamon

2 tbsp stevia

100 g / 3 ½ oz / ¾ cup walnut pieces

75 g / 2 ½ oz / ⅓ cup reduced fat baking spread

75 g / 2 ½ oz / ½ cup wholemeal flour

40 g / 1 ½ oz / ¼ cup coconut sugar

50 g / 1 ¾ oz / ½ cup rolled porridge oats

METHOD

1. Mix the strawberries and apple with the plain flour, cinnamon and stevia in a slow cooker.

2. Put the walnuts in a food processor and blitz until coarsely ground. Add the baking spread, flour and sugar and pulse until the mixture resembles fine breadcrumbs. Stir in the oats.

3. Take a handful of the topping and squeeze it into a clump, then crumble it over the fruit. Repeat with the rest of the crumble mixture and level the surface.

4. Cover and cook on high for 2 hours. Serve warm.

Sweet potato dessert

SERVES: 4 | PREP TIME: 10 MINUTES | COOKING TIME: 3 HOURS

INGREDIENTS

900 g / 2 lb / 7 cups sweet potatoes, peeled and diced

1 tsp ground cinnamon

1 tsp ground ginger

¼ tsp nutmeg, freshly grated

2 tbsp stevia

2 tbsp maple syrup

50 g / 1 ¾ oz / ¼ cup reduced fat baking spread

50 g / 1 ¾ oz / ⅓ cup pecan nuts, chopped

75 g / 2 ½ oz / 1 ¼ cups mini marshmallows

METHOD

1. Put the sweet potatoes in a slow cooker with the cinnamon, ginger, nutmeg, stevia, ½ a teaspoon of salt and 100 ml of water.

2. Cover and cook on high for 4 hours, stirring halfway through.

3. Add the maple syrup and baking spread and mash with a potato masher until smooth.

4. Scrape the mixture into a baking dish and top with pecan nuts and marshmallows.

5. Toast under a hot grill for a few minutes to brown before serving.

188

Bread and butter pudding

SERVES: 6 | PREP TIME: 20 MINUTES | COOKING TIME: 3 HOURS

INGREDIENTS

8 slices white bread

2 tbsp low fat spread

6 Medjool dates, stoned and torn into pieces

75 g / 2 ½ oz / ⅓ cup dried cranberries

400 ml / 14 fl. oz / 1 ⅔ cups skimmed milk

3 large eggs

1 tsp ground cinnamon

2 tbsp stevia

METHOD

1. Put a rack inside a slow cooker and add 2.5 cm (1 in) of boiling water, then set it to high. Grease a baking dish that will fit inside the slow cooker.

2. Spread the bread with low fat spread then tear into pieces and toss with the dates and cranberries in the baking dish. Whisk the milk with the eggs, cinnamon and stevia and pour it over the bread.

3. Cover the pudding with buttered foil, then transfer the dish to the slow cooker. Cover and cook on high for 3 hours or until set with just a slight wobble in the middle.

Peach crumbles

SERVES: 4 | PREP TIME: 15 MINUTES | COOKING TIME: 1 HOUR

INGREDIENTS

1 eating apple, peeled, cored and grated

50 ml / 1 ¾ fl. oz / ¼ cup coconut oil, melted

2 tbsp runny honey

50 g / 1 ¾ oz / ⅓ cup plain (all-purpose) flour

25 g ground almonds

50 g / 1 ¾ oz / ½ cup rolled porridge oats

4 under-ripe peaches, halved and stoned

1 tsp ground cinnamon

mint leaves, to garnish

METHOD

1. Preheat the oven to 160°C (140° fan) / 325F / gas 3.

2. Mix the grated apple with the coconut oil and honey, then stir in the flour, almonds and oats.

3. Shape the mixture into eight balls and press into the peach cavities. Arrange the peaches in a snug single layer in a baking dish and sprinkle with cinnamon.

4. Bake the peaches for 1 hour or until the crumble topping is golden and the peaches are tender to the point of a knife. Serve garnished with mint.

Pecan pie

SERVES: 8 | PREP TIME: 45 MINUTES | COOKING TIME: 4 HOURS

INGREDIENTS

100 g / 3 ½ oz / ½ cup reduced fat baking spread, cubed and chilled

200 g / 7 oz / 1 ⅓ cups plain (all-purpose) flour

3 large egg whites

150 g / 5 ½ oz / ½ cup runny honey

30 g cornflour (cornstarch)

1 tsp vanilla extract

1 tsp ground cinnamon

½ tsp nutmeg, freshly grated

200 g / 7 oz / 1 ⅔ cups pecan halves

METHOD

1. Rub the baking spread into the flour until the mixture resembles fine breadcrumbs. Stir in just enough cold water to bring the pastry together into a pliable dough, then chill for 30 minutes.

2. Roll out the pastry and use it to line a round tart tin that will fit snugly inside your slow cooker. Cover and cook on high for 1 hour.

3. Whisk the egg whites with the honey, then the cornflour, vanilla, cinnamon and nutmeg. Scrape the mixture into the pastry case and top with the pecans. Cover the slow cooker with a clean tea towel, followed by the lid, and cook on low for 3 hours.

191

Skinny cookies

SERVES: 12 | PREP TIME: 15 MINUTES | CHILL: 30 MINUTES | COOKING TIME: 4 HOURS

INGREDIENTS

100 g / 3 ½ oz / ½ cup coconut sugar

50 g / 1 ¾ oz / ¼ cup stevia

75 g / 2 ½ oz / ⅓ cup reduced fat
baking spread, softened

1 tsp vanilla extract

1 medium egg

125 g / 4 ½ oz / ¾ cup self-raising wholemeal flour

50 g / 1 ¾ oz / ⅓ cup 100 % cacao baking chips

METHOD

1. Cream the coconut sugar and stevia with the
butter and vanilla extract until pale and well
whipped then beat in the egg, followed by
the flour and cacao chips. Chill in the fridge
for 30 minutes or until stiff enough to shape.

2. Line a large slow cooker with greaseproof paper.

3. Divide the cookie dough into twelve balls
and space six of them out in the slow cooker.

4. Cover and cook on high for 2 hours
or until the cookies are set, but will still take
the imprint of your finger in the centre.

5. Transfer to a wire rack to cool
and repeat with the rest of the cookie dough.

Strawberry crumble

SERVES: 4-6 | PREP TIME: 15 MINUTES | COOKING TIME: 1 HOURS

••••••••••••••••••••••••

INGREDIENTS

500 g / 1 lb 1 oz strawberries

1 tbsp date syrup

2 tsp vanilla extract

150 g / 5 ¼ oz / 1 ½ cups ground almonds

75 g / 2 ½ oz / ⅓ cup unsalted butter, cold

25 g / 1 oz demerara sugar

100 g / 3 ½ oz / 1 ⅓ cups flaked (slivered) almonds

METHOD

1. Preheat the oven to 180°C (160°C fan) / 350F / gas 4.

2. Dehull and halve the strawberries and mix with the syrup and vanilla extract in a bowl. Sprinkle over 25 g of the ground almonds and place into a suitably sized ovenproof dish.

3. Place the remaining ground almonds in a clean mixing bowl and rub in cubes of the cold butter until the mixture resembles breadcrumbs.

4. Sprinkle the topping over the fruit and scatter the sugar and flaked almonds over the top.

5. Place into the oven and bake for 1 hour until golden on top and the fruit filling is hot and the juices are bubbling through.

6. Serve with low fat cream and fresh strawberries as desired.

Cinnamon and apple cake

SERVES: 4-6 | PREP TIME: 15 MINUTES | COOKING TIME: 1 HOUR

INGREDIENTS

75 g / 2 ½ oz / ⅓ cup unsalted butter

200 g / 7 oz / 1 ⅓ cups self-raising flour

100 g / 3 ½ oz / ½ cup coconut sugar

2 tsp ground cinnamon

350 g / 12 ¼ oz cooking apples, peeled and chopped

3 eggs, beaten

1 tbsp demerara sugar

METHOD

1. Preheat the oven to 180°C (160°C fan) / 350F / gas 4 and lightly grease an ovenproof dish.

2. Rub together the butter and flour until the mixture resembles breadcrumbs, add the sugar and mix through.

3. Place the cinnamon and apples into a saucepan and gently heat until the apples have started to break down. Set aside to cool.

4. Once cooled mix the apples and eggs into the dry ingredients to make a cake batter.

5. Pour into the prepared dish and sprinkle over the demerara sugar.

6. Bake in the oven for approximately 1 hour, until the top is crisp and the cake has started to come away from the edges and the centre of the cake is firm to the touch.

7. Remove from the oven and allow to cool slightly before serving. Can also be served cold.

Blueberry cheesecake with crumble topping

SERVES: 4-6 | PREP TIME: 20 MINUTES | COOKING TIME: 1 HOUR

INGREDIENTS

100 g / 3 ½ oz pecan nuts

100 g / 3 ½ oz Medjool dates

100 g / 3 ½ oz almond butter

200 g / 7 oz / 1 ⅓ cups blueberries

450 g / 15 ¾ oz low-fat cream cheese

150 g / 5 ¼ oz / ⅔ cup xylitol

1 tsp vanilla extract

4 eggs

75 g / 2 ½ oz / ¾ cup ground almonds

25 g / 1 oz unsalted butter, cold

METHOD

1. Preheat the oven to 160°C (140°C fan) / 325F / gas 3. Lightly grease a 23cm / 9 inch cake tin.

2. Place the nuts, dates and almond butter into a blender and blend until smooth. Press into the base of the cake tin.

3. Place the blueberries on top of the base of the cake.

4. Beat together the cheese, xylitol, vanilla extract and eggs until pale and creamy. Pour over the blueberries.

5. Rub together the ground almonds and butter until the mixture resembles breadcrumbs. Spoon over the top of the cake.

6. Bake in the oven for 1 hour at which point the cake should be set and topping lightly coloured. Remove from the oven and allow to cool for 12-15 minutes before carefully removing from the tin.

Spiced rhubarb

SERVES: 6 | PREP TIME: 5 MINUTES | COOKING TIME: 2 HOURS

INGREDIENTS

800 g / 1 lb 12 ½ oz forced rhubarb

2 star anise

1 cinnamon stick

1 vanilla pod, halved lengthways

3 slices fresh root ginger

50 g / 1 ¾ oz / ¼ cup stevia

METHOD

1. Cut the rhubarb into short lengths and put it in a slow cooker with the spices.

2. Sprinkle over the stevia and 3 tablespoons of water, then cover and cook on medium for 2 hours.

3. Serve warm or leave to cool completely before chilling in the fridge.

Plum cake

SERVES: 8-10 | PREP TIME: 15 MINUTES | COOKING TIME: 1 HOUR

INGREDIENTS

150 g / 5 ¼ oz / ⅔ cup xylitol

100 g / 3 ½ oz / ½ cup unsalted butter

150 g / 5 ¼ oz / 1 cup plain (all purpose) flour

1 tsp baking powder

2 eggs

12 plums, pitted and halved

METHOD

1. Preheat the oven to 160°C (140°C fan) / 325F / gas 3.

2. Beat the xylitol and butter together until pale and creamy.

3. Sift the flour and baking powder into the butter mixture and mix to combine. Add the eggs and mix into a smoother batter.

4. Place the plums into the bottom of a square cake tin. Pour over the cake batter.

5. Bake in the oven for 1 hour until risen and golden and a skewer placed into the centre of the cake comes out clean.

Crème brûlée

SERVES: 6 | PREP TIME: 30 MINUTES | COOKING TIME: 3 HOURS

INGREDIENTS

600 ml / 1 pint / 2 ½ cups skimmed milk

1 vanilla pod, halved lengthways

6 large egg yolks

1 tbsp stevia

2 tbsp icing (confectioner's) sugar

METHOD

1. Put the milk and vanilla pod in a small saucepan and bring slowly to a simmer.

2. Whisk the egg yolks and stevia together. Discard the vanilla pod then whisk in the hot milk. Pour the custard into 6 ramekins or bowls and cover the tops with foil.

3. Pour 2.5 cm (1 in) of water into the slow cooker, then arrange the ramekins in layers on racks. Cook on low for 3 hours or until the custards are just set with a slight wobble in the centre. Remove the ramekins from the slow cooker and chill for 4 hours.

4. Sprinkle with icing sugar and caramelise with a blowtorch or grill.

202

Mulled wine pears

SERVES: 6 | PREP TIME: 5 MINUTES | COOKING TIME: 2 HOURS

• •

INGREDIENTS

6 pears, peeled and cored

2 tbsp stevia

750 ml / 1 pint 5 ½ fl. oz / 3 cups red wine

4 dried orange slices

3 star anise

4 cloves

METHOD

1. Put all of the ingredients in a small slow cooker, then cover and cook on medium for 2 hours, turning the pears half way through.

2. Serve the pears in small glass jars, warm or chilled.

203

Plum streusel

SERVES: 8 | PREP TIME: 30 MINUTES | COOKING TIME: 2 HOURS, 30 MINUTES

INGREDIENTS

225 g / 8 oz / 1 ½ cups self raising flour

100 g / 3 ½ oz / ½ cup reduced fat baking spread, cubed and chilled

50 g / 1 ¾ oz / ¼ cup stevia

1 large egg

1 tsp vanilla extract

75 ml / 2 ½ fl. oz / ⅓ cup skimmed milk

low calorie cooking spray

FOR THE TOPPING

450 g / 1 lb / 3 cups plums, peeled, stoned and chopped

2 tbsp stevia

1 tsp ground cinnamon

75 g / 2 ½ oz / ¾ cup rolled oats

100 g / 3 ½ oz / ¾ cup hazelnuts

50 g / 1 ¾ oz / ¼ cup coconut sugar

2 tbsp coconut oil, melted

icing (confectioner's) sugar, for dusting

METHOD

1. Sieve the flour into a mixing bowl and rub in the baking spread until it resembles fine breadcrumbs then stir in the stevia. Lightly beat the egg with the vanilla and milk and stir it into the dry ingredients until just combined.

2. Grease the inside of a small slow cooker with cooking spray, then scrape in the cake mixture and level the surface.

3. Cover the slow cooker with a clean tea towel, then put the lid on and bake on medium for 1 hour 30 minutes.

4. Meanwhile, put the plums, stevia and cinnamon in a saucepan. Cook over a medium heat for 15 minutes or until reduced to a thick compote.

5. Put the oats, hazelnuts, coconut sugar and coconut oil in a food processor and pulse until finely chopped.

6. Spoon the plums on top of the cake and sprinkle over the streusel topping. Cover with the tea towel and lid again and cook for 1 hour. Leave to cool completely before dusting with icing sugar and cutting into slices.

7. Delicious served with pouring cream.

Almond biscotti

MAKES: 24 | PREP TIME: 20 MINUTES | COOKING TIME: 3 HOURS

INGREDIENTS

2 large eggs

50 g / 1 ¾ oz / ¼ cup reduced fat baking spread, melted

1 orange, zest finely grated

½ tsp vanilla extract

225 g / 8 oz / 1 ½ cups self-raising flour

50 g / 1 ¾ oz / ¼ cup stevia

100 g / 3 ½ oz / 1 cup whole almonds

METHOD

1. Preheat a large oval slow cooker to high and line it with a sheet of greaseproof paper.

2. Beat the eggs, baking spread, orange zest and vanilla together then stir in the flour, stevia and almonds.

3. Shape the dough into two long rolls and transfer them to the slow cooker. Cover and cook for 1 hour 30 minutes, then lift out the rolls with the greaseproof paper and leave to cool for 15 minutes.

4. Cut the rolls across into 1.5 cm (½ in) slices. Spread a single layer of slices out in the slow cooker, then leave the lid slightly ajar and cook for 45 minutes or until crisp. Repeat with the rest of the slices in batches until they are all cooked.

5. Leave to cool completely before serving.

Chocolate and banana loaf cake

SERVES: 8 | PREP TIME: 25 MINUTES | COOKING TIME: 2 HOURS

INGREDIENTS

4 very ripe bananas

110 g / 4 oz / ⅔ cup coconut sugar

2 large eggs

120 ml / 4 fl. oz / ½ cup sunflower oil

225 g / 8 oz / 1 ½ cups wholemeal flour

2 tbsp cacao powder

2 tsp baking powder

METHOD

1. Line a loaf tin that will fit inside your slow cooker with oiled greaseproof paper.

2. Mash three of the bananas with a fork then whisk in the sugar, eggs and oil.

3. Sieve the flour, baking powder and cacao into the bowl and stir just enough to evenly mix all the ingredients together. Slice the final banana and fold it in.

4. Spoon the mixture into the prepared tin and transfer it to the slow cooker. Cover the slow cooker with a clean tea towel, then put on the lid.

5. Cook on medium for 2 hours or until a skewer inserted into the centre of the cake comes out clean. Transfer the cake to a wire rack and leave to cool completely before cutting.

Blueberry crumble

SERVES: 6 | PREP TIME: 15 MINUTES | COOKING TIME: 2 HOURS

INGREDIENTS

450 g / 1 lb / 3 cups blueberries, plus extra to serve

1 tbsp plain (all-purpose) flour

2 tbsp stevia

75 g / 2 ½ oz / ⅓ cup reduced fat baking spread

75 g / 2 ½ oz / ½ cup wholemeal flour

40 g / 1 ½ oz / ¼ cup coconut sugar

50 g / 1 ¾ oz / ½ cup rolled porridge oats

METHOD

1. Mix the blueberries with the plain flour and stevia in a slow cooker.

2. Rub the baking spread into the wholemeal flour and stir in the sugar and oats. Take a handful of the topping and squeeze it into a clump, then crumble it over the fruit. Repeat with the rest of the crumble mixture and level the surface.

3. Cover and cook on high for 2 hours. The top can be coloured under a hot grill for a few minutes if you prefer.

4. Serve hot or cold with an extra sprinkle of fresh blueberries.

Stewed apples with pancakes

SERVES: 2 | PREP TIME: 10 MINUTES | COOKING TIME: 4 HOURS

INGREDIENTS

4 cooking apples, peeled, cored and chopped

50 g / 1 ¾ oz low fat spread

1 lemon, juiced

1 tsp cinnamon

50 g / 1 ¾ oz / ¼ cup coconut sugar

50 ml / 1 ¾ fl. oz / ¼ cup sugar free apple juice

100 g / 3 ½ oz / ⅔ cup plain (all-purpose) flour

50 g / 1 ¾ oz xylitol

1 egg

100 ml / 3 ½ fl. oz / ½ cup milk

low calorie cooking spray

METHOD

1. Place the apples, spread, lemon juice, cinnamon, coconut sugar and apple juice into a slow cooker. Cook on low for 4 hours.

2. Whisk together the flour, xylitol, egg and milk to make a smooth batter, the thickness of double cream.

3. Place a non-stick pan onto a medium heat and spray with cooking spray. Ladle the batter into the pan and spread evenly over the pan to form a thin pancake. Cook for 2-3 minutes before flipping and cooking for a further minute. Serve the pancakes with the stewed apples spooned over the top.

Poached apples with lingonberry jam

SERVES: 4 | PREP TIME: 5 MINUTES | COOKING TIME: 2 HOURS

INGREDIENTS

4 apples, peeled, cored and halved

500 ml / 17 ½ fl. oz / 2 cups apple juice

1 star anise

1 cinnamon stick

4 cloves

100 ml / 3 ½ fl. oz / ½ cup lingonberry jam (jelly)

METHOD

1. Arrange the apples cut side down in a single layer in a slow cooker, then add the juice and spices.

2. Cook on medium for 2 hours or until the apples are tender to the point of a knife.

3. Fill the cavity of each apple with jam and serve warm or chilled.

Lemon yogurt cakes

SERVES: 6 | PREP TIME: 20 MINUTES | COOKING TIME: 2 HOURS

INGREDIENTS

125 ml / 4 ½ fl. oz / ½ cup sunflower oil

75 g / 2 ½ oz / ⅓ cup stevia

1 lemon, juiced and zest finely grated, plus a little extra zest to garnish

3 large eggs

125 ml / 4 ½ fl. oz / ½ cup low fat natural yogurt

150 g / 5 ½ oz / 1 cup self-raising flour

icing (confectioner's) sugar for sprinkling

METHOD

1. Put a rack in the bottom of a slow cooker and add 2.5 cm (1 in) of boiling water. Grease six individual ramekins or gratin dishes.

2. Measure the oil, sugar, lemon juice and zest, eggs and yogurt into a mixing bowl and whisk together until smoothly combined. Fold in the flour. Divide the mixture between the ramekins, then layer them up in the slow cooker, on racks if necessary. Cook on high for 2 hours or until a skewer inserted in the centre comes out clean.

3. Transfer the cakes to a wire rack and leave to cool a little before serving sprinkled with icing sugar and lemon zest.

Berry clafoutis

SERVES: 6 | PREP TIME: 25 MINUTES | COOKING TIME: 3 HOUR

INGREDIENTS

low calorie baking spray

50 g / 1 ¾ oz / ⅓ cup plain (all purpose) flour

50 g / 1 ¾ oz / ¼ cup stevia

2 tbsp ground almonds

300 ml / 10 ½ fl. oz / 1 ¼ cups skimmed milk

2 large eggs

2 tbsp reduced fat baking spread, melted

150 g / 5 ½ oz / 1 cup strawberries, cut into quarters

150 g / 5 ½ oz / 1 cup blueberries

icing (confectioner's) sugar for dusting

METHOD

1. Spray the inside of a small slow cooker with low calorie baking spray.

2. Whisk together the milk and eggs with the melted baking spread.

3. Sift the flour into a mixing bowl with a pinch of salt, then stir in the ground almonds and stevia.

4. Make a well in the middle of the dry ingredients and gradually whisk in the liquid.

5. Arrange half the strawberries and blueberries in the slow cooker then pour over the batter.

6. Cover the slow cooker with a tea towel, followed by the lid.

7. Cook on low for 3 hours.

8. Serve the clafoutis hot or cold, garnished with the rest of the berries and a sprinkle of icing sugar.

Cranberry crumbles

SERVES: 4 | PREP TIME: 15 MINUTES | COOKING TIME: 2 HOURS

INGREDIENTS

450 g / 1 lb / 3 cups cranberries, plus a few
extra to serve

1 tbsp plain (all-purpose) flour

50 g / 1 ¾ oz / ¼ cup stevia

75 g / 2 ½ oz / ⅓ cup reduced fat baking spread

75 g / 2 ½ oz / ½ cup wholemeal flour

40 g coconut sugar

100 g / 3 ½ oz / 1 cup rolled porridge oats

METHOD

1. Mix the cranberries with the plain flour and
   stevia and divide between four large mugs
   that will fit inside your slow cooker in a
   single layer.

2. Rub the baking spread into the wholemeal
   flour and stir in the sugar and oats.
   Take a handful of the topping. Squeeze it
   into a clump, then crumble it into the first
   mug. Repeat with the rest of the crumble
   mixture, alternating between the mugs.

3. Pour 2.5 cm (1 in) boiling water into the slow
   cooker and put the mugs inside.
   Cover and cook on high for 2 hours.

4. Serve hot or cold, topped with a few extra
   fresh cranberries.

Chocolate, coffee and walnut cake

SERVES: 8 | PREP TIME: 20 MINUTES | COOKING TIME: 1 HOUR, 30 MINUTES

INGREDIENTS

125 g / 4 ½ oz / ½ cup stevia

200 g / 7 oz / ¾ cup reduced fat baking spread

4 large eggs

1 tsp baking powder

2 tbsp cacao powder, plus extra for dusting

1 tbsp instant espresso powder

2 tbsp skimmed milk

75 g / 2 ½ oz / ½ cup dark chocolate
(min. 70 % cocoa solids), chopped

75 g / 2 ½ oz / ⅔ cup walnuts, finely chopped

METHOD

1. Grease the inside of small round slow cooker, preferably 20 cm (8 inches) in diameter, and line it with greaseproof paper.

2. Put the flour, stevia, baking spread, eggs, baking powder, cacao, espresso powder and milk in a bowl and whisk with an electric whisk for 3 minutes or until well-whipped. Fold in the chocolate and walnuts.

3. Scrape the mixture into the slow cooker and cover with a clean tea towel, followed by the lid.

4. Cook on high for 1 hour 30 minutes or until a skewer inserted in the centre comes out clean.

5. Turn the cake out onto a wire rack and leave to cool completely before dusting the top with cacao.

Raspberry sponge cake

SERVES: 10 | PREP TIME: 45 MINUTES | COOKING TIME: 1 HOUR, 30 MINUTES

INGREDIENTS

200 g / 7 oz / 1 ⅓ cups self-raising flour

125 g / 4 ½ oz / ½ cup stevia

200 g / 7 oz / ¾ cup reduced fat baking spread

4 large eggs

1 tsp baking powder

1 tsp vanilla extract

TO DECORATE

100 ml / 3 ½ fl. oz / ½ cup diabetic raspberry jam (jelly)

300 ml / 10 ½ fl. oz / 1 ¼ cups 0% fat Greek yogurt

150 g / 5 ½ oz / 1 cup raspberries

icing (confectioner's) sugar, for dusting

METHOD

1. Grease the inside of small round slow cooker, preferably 20 cm (8 inches) in diameter, and line it with greaseproof paper.

2. Put all of the cake ingredients in a bowl and whisk with an electric whisk for 3 minutes or until well-whipped.

3. Scrape the mixture into the slow cooker and cover with a clean tea towel, followed by the lid. Cook on high for 1 hour 30 minutes or until a skewer inserted in the centre comes out clean. Turn the cake out onto a wire rack and leave to cool completely.

4. Cut the cake in half horizontally and transfer the base to a serving plate. Top with jam and yogurt and scatter over the berries.

5. Put the other half of the cake on top and dust lightly with icing sugar.

INDEX